The Life of Walatta-Petros

The Life of Walatta-Petros

A SEVENTEENTH-CENTURY BIOGRAPHY
OF AN AFRICAN WOMAN

CONCISE EDITION

TRANSLATED AND EDITED BY

Wendy Laura Belcher and Michael Kleiner

WRITTEN BY GALAWDEWOS

PRINCETON UNIVERSITY PRESS
PRINCETON AND OXFORD

Published by Princeton University Press
41 William Street, Princeton, New Jersey 08540
6 Oxford Street, Woodstock, Oxfordshire OX20 1TR

press.princeton.edu

This book includes material originally published in *The Life and Struggles of Our Mother Walatta Petros: A Seventeenth-Century Biography of an Ethiopian Woman* (copyright © 2015 by Princeton University Press).

Cover art: Walatta Petros counting the hippo's teeth on Lake Tana (SLUB Dresden / Digital Collections / 3.A.6718)

Library of Congress Control Number 2018935646
ISBN 978-0-691-18291-9

British Library Cataloging-in-Publication Data is available

This book has been composed in Linux Libertine 0

Printed on acid-free paper. ∞

Printed in the United States of America

1 3 5 7 9 10 8 6 4 2

❧ CONTENTS ❧

❧ INTRODUCTION ❧

Wendy Laura Belcher

When I, one of the translators of this book, was four years old, my American family moved from rainy Seattle, Washington, to the highland city of Gondar, Ethiopia, so that my physician father could teach at a small medical college there. Over the next three years, I began to learn about the many facets of this East African country. You need to learn about them, too, if you are to understand the book you hold in your hands.

Flying low over the green Ethiopian countryside, I saw the thatched roofs of many round adobe churches. I visited a cathedral carved three stories down into the stone. I awoke most mornings to the sound of priests chanting. I learned that the peoples of highland Eritrea and Ethiopia, who call themselves the Habasha, are Christians and have been Christians for approximately seventeen hundred years, longer than most European peoples. Their church is called the Ethiopian Orthodox Church: it is not Roman Catholic, Protestant, or Eastern Orthodox. It is a special form of Christianity called non-Chalcedonian, and ancient churches in Egypt, Eritrea, Syria, Armenia, and India share many beliefs with them. The Ethiopian Orthodox Church reveres saints, about three hundred of whom are Habasha men and women who were especially holy leaders.

The college gatekeeper in Gondar patiently taught me how to write some of the several hundred characters of the traditional Ethiopian script, which looked nothing like the Latin or Roman alphabet I was studying in school. For instance, to write the sound *qo* you use the character ቆ, or to write the sound *bu* you use the character ቡ. I learned that the Habasha had been writing in the ancient African script and language of Gəʿəz (ግዕዝ) for almost two thousand years. The Habasha have used this ancient language for many centuries to conduct worship in their church services, to translate Christian and secular literature from elsewhere, and to write original texts of theology, poetry, saints' lives, and history.

Hiking from our home in Gondar up the steep mountainside to an eighteenth-century stone castle, I saw men bent over their laps writing with cane pens on animal skin, called parchment. These scribes were monks who lived in one of the thousand Habasha monasteries. Habasha scribes have been producing bound manuscripts since at least the sixth century, many with lavish illustrations known as illuminations. These scribes ensured that their church and monastic libraries were rich in the most important texts, whether translations from other languages or original compositions in Gəʿəz, by copying important manuscripts from other churches and monasteries, preserving them without printing presses or cameras. Perhaps only a quarter of the manuscripts in these monastic libraries have been cataloged, much less digitized, so many of their riches are largely unknown outside their walls.

In other words, I learned at an early age that the Christianity, language, and books of Ethiopia and Eritrea had nothing to do with Europe. The book you hold in your hands will make sense if you, too, remember all this.

I introduce the book with these points because when I tell people that this book was written in Africa long ago, in 1672, their preconceptions often do not allow them to understand me. They simply cannot conceive that Africans were reading and writing books hundreds of years ago, or that some black peoples were both literate and Christian before some white peoples. They say things to me like, "Wait, what European wrote this book?" or "Wait, in what European language was this book written?" Sometimes they even correct me: "Oh, I think you mean it was written in 1972." So let me say it clearly: This book was written almost three hundred and fifty years ago, by Africans, for Africans, in an African language, about African Christianity. It was not written by Europeans.

This book is an extraordinary true story about Ethiopia but also about early modern African women's lives, leadership, and passions—full of vivid dialogue, heartbreak, and triumph. Indeed, it is the earliest-known book-length biography of an Ethiopian or African woman.

Historical and Religious Context of the Book

In the 1500s and early 1600s, Roman Catholic Jesuit missionaries traveled to highland Ethiopia to urge the Habasha to convert from their ancient form of African Christianity to Roman Catholicism. The Jesuits ultimately failed, in part due to their cultural insensitivity. They did not blame themselves, however. They blamed their failure instead on the Habasha noblewomen.

When I first read this accusation, I thought that it was simple misogyny: sure, blame the women! But the more I read, the more I began to understand that one of the earliest European efforts to colonize Africa did indeed fail in part because of African women. Many Habasha men of the court converted for reasons of state, but their mothers, wives, and daughters mostly did not. These women fought the Europeans with everything they had—from vigorous debate to outright murder—and after a decade, the Habasha men joined them. Together, they banished all Europeans from the country. Indeed, Ethiopia became one of the few countries never to be colonized by Europeans.

The Christianity of the Habasha is different from that of the Protestants and Roman Catholics. First, their Christianity is very ascetic, meaning it is against worldly pleasures. It holds that weakening the body reduces desires and thus leads to purity. Fasting is very important; many Habasha abstain from eating animal products half of the days of the year. Monks and nuns go further, eating only one meal on those days. The faithful often engage in other ascetic practices as well, such as praying while standing in cold water, staying up all night in prayer, or living in caves. Second, the Ethiopian Orthodox Church has a doctrine of *theosis*, the transformation of human beings by grace. This doctrine means that human beings are not inevitably sinful but actually have the potential of becoming without sin, like the Virgin Mary, Jesus's mother. As a result, the ultimate goal of Habasha monks and nuns is to leave the human behind, in part by reducing the body's desires to nothing. When reading this book, you will see many instances of human asceticism and holiness.

Some other attributes that the Ethiopian Orthodox Church shares with other churches include a deep reverence for the Virgin Mary—the pious recite prayers in her honor every day, and most church services include readings of her miracles—and a system of monasticism that began in Egypt in the early days of Christianity. Their monasteries do not have one overarching authority but are largely autonomous, with their own rules and procedures. Also, a monastery is not inextricably tied to a particular monastic building or church edifice but is a community marked by its practices of asceticism, celibacy, education, and preaching the Gospel. When reading this book, you will see many references to Mary and monasticism.

Biography of Walatta-Petros

This book is about one of the Habasha women who refused to convert to Roman Catholicism when its missionaries came to highland Ethiopia. Her name is Walatta-Petros, which means "Daughter of Saint Peter" (this is a compound name and can never be shortened to "Walatta" or "Petros," just as you would never shorten "Peterson" to "Peter" or "Son"). She was born in 1592 into a wealthy, noble family, and she died in 1642 at the age of fifty. Walatta-Petros resisted converting to European forms of Christianity, and she and her sisters helped inspire a nation to do the same.

Walatta-Petros might seem to be unique. She was, after all, a literate seventeenth-century African woman. She was an important leader, directing a successful nonviolent movement against Europeans. She founded her own monastery, over which she presided without any male authority over her. Her Ethiopian disciples wrote a book about her. Yet closer examination reveals that Walatta-Petros is not exceptional but exemplary. That is, she is not a uniquely strong African woman but an example of millions of strong ones. Many assume that Africa is the continent where women have been the most abused, yet Walatta-Petros is just one woman in Africa's long tradition of strong ruling queens, legally independent and literate noblewomen, and female deities and saints. Evidence from multiple sources in multiple languages demonstrates that African women like Walatta-Petros were essential to the histories of their nations.

After being raised in an adoring family, Walatta-Petros was married to a powerful man named Malkiya-Kristos, one of the king's most important counselors and military commanders. He decided to convert to Roman Catholicism, along with the king and other noblemen, but Walatta-Petros was against the "filthy faith of the foreigners," as the text puts it. She decided to leave her husband and take up the life of a nun around the age of twenty-three, in part because all three of her children had died in infancy, leaving married life without its fruits. Her husband threatened to destroy an entire town to retrieve her, so Walatta-Petros returned to her husband to save the townspeople from death. However, when she learned that her husband had participated in killing the head of the Ethiopian Orthodox Church, she withdrew from him in disgust, abandoning his bed, all forms of adornment, and eating. Finally, her husband allowed her to leave him and fulfill her dream of becoming a nun.

Within a few days, Walatta-Petros met another noblewoman who was becoming a nun and also resisting Roman Catholic conversion. This fellow nun, Eheta-Kristos (meaning "Sister of Christ"), became Walatta-Petros's lifelong partner and companion, and you will read a lot about her in the book.

Walatta-Petros then began her life as a radical itinerant preacher. She publicly rebuked all those who had converted—including the king, his court, and the clergy. She became an enemy of the state and regularly had to flee persecution, with such high-ranking figures as the king's brother and second-in-command, Silla-Kristos, hunting her down. Enraged by her behavior, the king ordered that she appear before the entire court—all its princes, governors, officials, and scholars—a sign of what a threat she was considered. She was so fearless there that her husband had to beg the king to spare her life, which he did.

Walatta-Petros's fame skyrocketed after her confrontation with the king, and many of the Habasha faithful came long distances to join her emphatically Orthodox, and therefore decidedly anti-Catholic, religious community. As revolutionaries, Walatta-Petros's followers had to move constantly to new towns and regions to stay ahead of the king's spies and the European soldiers who wanted to kill them. Soon Walatta-Petros was hauled before the court again, but her husband again saved her life by suggesting that the king subject her to thought reform. The king agreed, and a team of Roman Catholic priests spent every Saturday with her, working to convert her to Roman Catholicism. They were not successful. Every week the king would ask the European head of the Roman Catholics whether he had succeeded, and every week he had to report that he had not. Walatta-Petros resisted one of the most persuasive educational institutions ever invented. When all these efforts failed, the king made up his mind to kill her, but yet again her husband saved her life by suggesting another compromise: exile. So the king banished her to a place on the edge of their known world, where she was kept in chains among the "pagans." Her jailer tried to seduce and then kill her, but she did not succumb and instead survived. Eventually, struck by the force of her convictions, he became a devotee. By special dispensation, the king allowed her to return then, after three years in the wilderness, along with all those who had followed her there.

When Walatta-Petros returned to highland Ethiopia, she established her religious community in and around Lake Tana, a huge lake with many monasteries. She was the head of her community; there was no abbot in charge over her. Unsurprisingly, she encountered strong resistance from local male leaders, who challenged her authority and asked where in the Bible it said that a woman could lead and preach. A famous monk and scholar defended her, however, saying that God raised up a woman to defend the Ethiopian Orthodox Church because many priests had abandoned it.

Not long after, in 1632, the king rescinded his edict making Roman Catholicism the state religion, and the country returned to the beliefs of the Ethiopian Orthodox Church. Walatta-Petros was elevated by her people as a heroine who had helped enable the return of the true church. She spent the remaining twelve years of her life traveling and setting up religious communities in new towns. The events of this latter part of her life take up more than half the book. She performed many miracles and saved her community from repeated threats, sometimes with drastic measures (Walatta-Petros is not a "nice" saint), but only growing in reputation. She died after an unknown illness that lasted several months, having lived twenty-six years as a nun. After her death, her community set up a monastery devoted to her at Qoratsa (now Qorata), on the eastern shore of Lake Tana. There, Eheta-Kristos became the abbess of Walatta-Petros's monastery until her own death. That monastery still exists today.

The Writing of This Book

Thirty years after Walatta-Petros died, the young monk Galawdewos wrote a beautiful book about her life, based on the community's oral histories. Many of the stories told about Walatta-Petros are told by women, so this book is not just about an African woman but is written in part *by* African women. Titled ገድለ፡ወለተ፡ ጴጥሮስ (*Gädlä Wälättä Ṗeṭros* [*Life-Struggles of Walatta-Petros*]), this book is in a genre called a hagiography, or saint's life. About one hundred Habasha saints have had hagiographies written about them. Only five of those books, including this one, have been translated into English, and the other four translations are difficult to access. Meanwhile, only one translation into English of the hagiography of any black female saint—the seventeenth-century West African Spanish saint Teresa Chicaba—has been published, and it was written by Europeans, not Africans. Our translation represents the first accessible translation into English of an early modern African woman's life.

Because this book is a hagiography, it cannot be read as a strictly factual historical source. Hagiographies are written to celebrate saints and religious belief. In them, saints sometimes raise people from the dead, heal the incurably ill, predict the future, and even fly. However, Walatta-Petros's hagiography is grounded in historical events. Both Walatta-Petros and her husband were real people who appear in European historical sources and the Habasha royal chronicles from the period. Also, this hagiography is remarkably detailed—filled with the names of specific historical people and places, and the precise verifiable dates when historical events occurred, in part because it was written close to the events and generally based on eyewitness accounts. Most of the text proceeds without any supernatural miracles. While you need to read this book carefully, as you have to read all sources, it does provide useful historical and cultural information. It is not only the earliest-known biography of an African woman but also an early account of resistance to European colonialism from an African perspective.

The Translation of This Book

Michael Kleiner, a German scholar of Gəʿəz literature and Ethiopian history, drafted a translation of this book, which he and I then collaboratively refined. We sought to produce an accessible and fluid English text while also remaining faithful to the Gəʿəz. This is not a loose, literary translation, and we did not add long phrases, full sentences, or paragraphs. We stayed as close as possible to the original in our full translation of every part of Walatta-Petros's hagiography, which we published in 2015, titled *The Life and Struggles of Our Mother Walatta Petros: A Seventeenth-Century African Biography of an Ethiopian Woman*. That is a rigorous scholarly publication of 544 pages with a wide-ranging introduction; rich, substantive notes; a comprehensive glossary of people, places, and concepts; the full cycle of twenty-seven miracles, two poems, and a community history that appear at the end of manuscripts; and dozens of vivid illustrations from the original manuscripts.

Our translation is based on consulting many manuscript copies (a complicated process described at length in the full edition)—one of which I believe is the original that Galawdewos wrote, which has been kept ever since in Walatta-Petros's monastery in highland Ethiopia. The other manuscripts are copies of that original, or copies of those copies. Thus, each manuscript is slightly different from the others due to copying errors or improvements. In the full edition of the book, we document the variations among these manuscripts in the notes.

We knew that the full edition was longer and more complex than most students or general readers would want to use, so we created this paperback edition, which is shorter and easier to read. It differs in the following ways from the full translation: First, we have included only the life of Walatta-Petros and one tale about a miracle she is reported to have performed after her death. The full translation includes poems celebrating her and twenty-six additional tales about the miracles she is reported to have performed after her death; you can read the poems online if you are interested. Second, we have added a few more explanatory terms for readers who might be unfamiliar with Ethiopian history and culture, changed some unfamiliar Gəʿəz terms to their English equivalents, and sometimes provided information in the main text that had been in footnotes. As a result, some words in the paperback translation did not actually appear in the original text or the full edition. Third, in the full edition we included many scholarly footnotes and a long glossary of all people, places, and terms. We removed all the notes and the glossary for this paperback edition, although you can consult the glossary online via the Princeton University Press website. Fourth, in the full edition, we clearly marked where we added any words not in the original Gəʿəz (using brackets) or where our translation was even a little bit free (in the notes). Those marks and notes have all been deleted from the paperback edition. The translation is the same, but how it varies from the original is not marked. Fifth, in the paperback edition, we took the opportunity to correct a few small oversights of the full edition, including some corrections of dates.

In both editions we often substituted a full English noun for a pronoun (e.g., translating "she replied to him" as "Walatta-Petros replied to Malkiya-Kristos"). We also created all of the chapter titles and their placement to make the text easier to read; they are not present in any form in the original text. You can find a full description of our principles of translation in the full edition, *The Life and Struggles of Our Mother Walatta Petros.*

For the Interested Student

If you are writing a paper about this book, that's wonderful. Few people have studied this book, despite its importance and beauty. You are now part of a vital effort to give this text the attention it deserves.

One way to arrive at ideas for a paper about this book is to ask: How does *The Life of Walatta-Petros* think about the world? That may seem a weird question—how can a book think?—but treating a book as something that thinks can help you get to significant insights.

- How does this text think about the divine? Who and what is divine and what is the relation of the divine to the human? What is prayer and how does it work?
- How does this text think about the human power to act? Do people control all their actions? Do they choose their fate?
- How does this text think about social status and rank? Who has power over others and who does not?
- How does this text think about leadership? Who is a leader and how do different leaders behave toward their followers? Do good leaders sacrifice individuals to save the community?
- How does this text think about friendship? Which people are friends and how do they treat each other?

- How does this text think about animals? Which animals are in the text, how do they behave, and what is their relation to human beings?
- How does this text think about gender? Do men and women act differently? If so, how? If not, why? Does this text think about gender in the same way that the people around you do?
- How does this text think about sexuality? In particular, how does the text think about celibacy, same-sex desire, or opposite-sex desire? But also, what is a family? How do husbands and wives or other types of partners behave toward each other?
- How does this text think about place? Where does Walatta-Petros travel and set up religious communities? What do we learn about those places? Is there a pattern to the movement of people in the text?
- How does this book think about other books? It quotes from more than forty biblical books. Why? Do words have power in the world? What do books mean to people in this book?
- How does this book think about authorship? Who is telling the stories in the book and how do they tell stories differently?
- How does this text think about Europeans and their role in this specific time and place in history? How does this text think about other foreigners or local ethnic groups?
- How does this text think about race?
- How does this book think about writing? That is, what does it value in terms of form and style, metaphors and tropes, discourse and language, the structure and order of material, and genre?

If you are interested in learning more about this book for your research, go online to the Princeton University Press website (http://press.princeton.edu/titles/10584.html). On the webpage for the original edition of this book, you will find links to the glossary, which provides information on each person, place, and term in the text, and the introduction from the full edition, which describes the historical, religious, cultural, and authorial contexts of the text. You will also find a link to the two poems about Walatta-Petros, with the original Gəʿəz and English translation side by side for better interpretation.

If you plan to do extended work on this text, either for a thesis or a publication, you will need to use the full edition of the book, which gives much more information on the twelve manuscripts we used, as well as on Gəʿəz philology, the Ethiopian script, our translation principles, and many other essential matters. It also includes many footnotes to aid scholars in interpreting the text and dozens of gorgeous seventeenth- and eighteenth-century illustrations of Walatta-Petros's life.

If you enjoy reading this book, you should know that Ethiopian studies is in need of young scholars to learn Gəʿəz and work to preserve, study, and translate the masterpieces of Ethiopian literature like this one. Please consider joining the cause! It won't be easy. Classes in Gəʿəz are few and far between, but learning the language will be a fun challenge—and the contribution you make will be priceless.

For Instructors

A lesson plan for teaching a unit on this book, including assignments, related articles, and a video, can be found at http://www.wendybelcher.com/african-literature/walatta-petros/#Lesson Plan.

Further Reading

To read the glossary of people, places, and terms; an introduction about the historical, cultural, and religious context; and the poems in honor of Walatta-Petros from the full edition of the *Gädlä Wälättä Petros*, see http://press.princeton.edu/titles/10584.html.

Belcher, Wendy Laura. "Same-Sex Intimacies in the Early African Text the *Gädlä Wälättä Petros* (1672): Queer Reading an Ethiopian Female Saint." *Research in African Literatures* 47, no. 2 (June 2016): 20–45.

————. "Sisters Debating the Jesuits: The Role of African Women in Defeating Portuguese Cultural Colonialism in Seventeenth-Century Abyssinia." *Northeast African Studies* 12 (Spring 2013): 121–66.

Bosc-Tiessé, Claire. "Creating an Iconographic Cycle: The Manuscript of the Acts of Wälättä Ṗeṭros and the Emergence of Qʷäraṭa as a Place of Asylum." In *Fifteenth International Conference of Ethiopian Studies*, edited by Siegbert Uhlig, 409–16. Wiesbaden: Harrassowitz, 2003.

Chernetsov, Sevir. "A Transgressor of the Norms of Female Behaviour in Seventeenth-Century Ethiopia: The Heroine of *The Life of Our Mother Walatta Petros*." *Khristianski Vostok* (*Journal of the Christian East*) 10 (2005): 48–64.

Galawdewos. *The Life and Struggles of Our Mother Walatta Petros: A Seventeenth-Century African Biography of an Ethiopian Woman*. Translated and edited by Wendy Laura Belcher and Michael Kleiner. Princeton, NJ: Princeton University Press, 2015.

Selamawit Mecca. "Hagiographies of Ethiopian Female Saints: With Special Reference to *Gädlä Krestos Sämra* and *Gädlä Feqertä Krestos*." *Journal of African Cultural Studies* 18, no. 2 (December 2006): 153–67.

❈ MAPS ❈

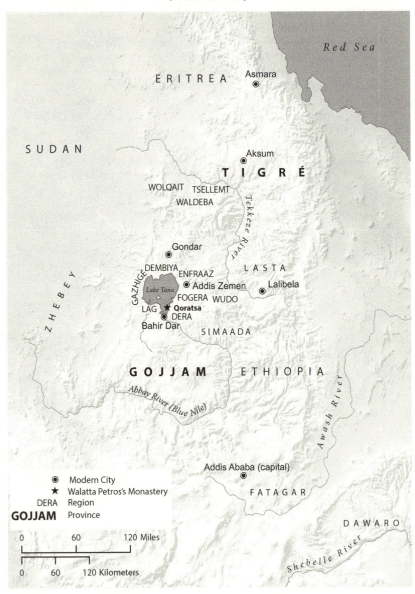

Map 1. Seventeenth-century regions in highland Ethiopia that Walatta-Petros visited.
Map by Tsering Wangyal Shawa.

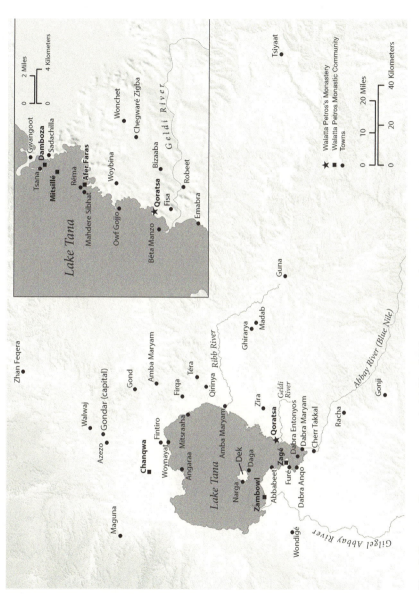

Map 2. Seventeenth-century towns in highland Ethiopia that Walatta-Petros visited. Map by Tsering Wangyal Shawa.

❧ CHRONOLOGY ❧

1557   Jesuits arrive in Ethiopia.

1592   Walatta-Petros is born to Bahir-Saggad and Kristos-Ebayaa.

1607   Susinyos becomes king.

1608   Walatta-Petros marries Malkiya-Kristos around this year.

1612   King Susinyos converts to Roman Catholicism.

1617   Walatta-Petros's husband participates in the murder of
        Patriarch Simeon.

1617   Walatta-Petros leaves her husband, meets Eheta-Kristos, and
        becomes a nun.

1621   King Susinyos forbids the teaching of Ethiopian Orthodoxy.

1622–32 Walatta-Petros travels, preaches, founds three communities,
        and is persecuted.

1632   Susinyos rescinds the edict forcing conversion to Roman
        Catholicism and dies; his son Fasiladas becomes king.

1632–42 Walatta-Petros founds and leads four more communities.

1642   Walatta-Petros falls ill in August and dies on November 23.

1642   Eheta-Kristos becomes abbess of Walatta-Petros's
        community.

1649   Eheta-Kristos dies on April 2.

1650   Walatta-Petros's community becomes an official monastery
        through a royal land grant.

1672–73 Galawdewos writes down the story of Walatta-Petros's life.

❀ PERSONALITIES ❀

For full information about the people in this book, see the book's page on the Princeton University Press website, which includes a link to a seventy-page glossary of people, places, and terms in the text.

Afonsu: The Portuguese Jesuit Afonso Mendes served in Ethiopia as the head of the Roman Catholic mission from 1625 to 1634.

Bahir-Saggad: Walatta-Petros's father, who died when she was young.

Billa-Kristos: King Susinyos's male cousin and confidant; a Roman Catholic convert.

Eheta-Kristos: A noblewoman who left her husband and daughter to become a nun. She then became Walatta-Petros's companion, served as a leader in her communities, and died on April 2, 1649.

Fasiladas: The Ethiopian king (1603–67) who came to power in 1632 and restored Ethiopian Orthodoxy after his father, King Susinyos, declared Catholicism the state religion in 1621.

Galawdewos: The author of the *Gädlä Wälättä Peṭros*; a novice monk and member of Walatta-Petros's monastery; he relates stories told to him by community members.

Kristos-Ebayaa: Walatta-Petros's mother, who materially supported Walatta-Petros's early community.

Malkiya-Kristos: Walatta-Petros's husband, a Roman Catholic convert, and chief adviser of King Susinyos.

Silla-Kristos: King Susinyos's half brother and head military enforcer of Roman Catholicism. Not to be confused with Father Silla-Kristos.

Simeon: An Egyptian, the head of the Ethiopian Orthodox Church from 1607 to 1617.

Susinyos: The king of Ethiopia from 1606 to 1632 and Walatta-Petros's sworn enemy. He declared Catholicism the state religion in 1621 and forbade Orthodox preaching and practice. This triggered a religious civil war, which ended in 1632 when he rescinded that edict.

Walatta-Petros: The subject of this book, a noblewoman (1592–1642) who resisted conversion to Roman Catholicism and led many who did the same.

Yohannes I: King of Ethiopia (r. 1667–82) when Walatta-Petros's hagiography was written.

The Life of Walatta-Petros

❦ THE TRANSLATION OF THE LIFE ❦ OF WALATTA-PETROS

Wendy Laura Belcher and Michael Kleiner

Note: We recommend that instructors assign this concise edition to students but use the full hardcover edition, *The Life and Struggles of Our Mother Walatta Petros*, themselves. Because the page numbers are different in both editions, this may cause confusion during classroom discussions of the text. Therefore, we have provided a cross-reference—the numbers in the margins of this concise edition refer to the corresponding page in the full hardcover edition. So, if you are a student and your instructor is using the hardcover edition and says, "turn to page 77," don't look at the page numbers at the top of your page in the concise edition but look at the page numbers in the left or right margin.

In the name of God, who was before all time and who will be for eternity, who is without beginning and without end! He is our Lord by virtue of his divinity and our Father by virtue of his benevolence. Our praise of him comes from him, and our glorification of him emanates from that which belongs to him. He is all-powerful; nothing is impossible for him. For eternity, amen. [77]

Introduction

I, the sinner and transgressor Galawdewos, will write a small part of the story of her persecution, as well as of the many struggles and virtuous deeds of our holy Mother Walatta-Petros, the mother-of-pearl, the mother of a myriad of precious stones, she of holy lips and mouth. Word of her deeds has spread throughout the world and has been proclaimed from one end to the other. Truly, this word benefits anyone who hears it, profits anyone who listens to it, and is a path to salvation for anyone who pursues and follows it. [78]

I now write this out of neither presumption nor pride, nor because I seek empty praise or vain accolades. Rather, I write it because the young nun Qiddista-Kristos, who burned with love for Walatta-Petros, made me do it, saying, "Write, so that Walatta-Petros's story may be known, so that it may reach those places that it has not yet reached, that anyone who has not yet heard it may hear it, and that her commemoration may be read by the generations of those who will come after us, in perpetuity!" As Christ says in the Gospel, "What I told you in the dark, proclaim in the light, and what I whispered in your ears, preach on the rooftops. A city built upon a hill cannot be hid. Neither do people light a lamp to then put it under a basket. Instead they will put it on a stand so that it gives light to everyone in the house."

Chapter 1: The Author's Worthiness

Because of Qiddista-Kristos's urging, I, too, became eager to follow this story from its beginning to its end. Even though I am not worthy to mention Walatta-Petros's name with my impure mouth or to write her story with my polluted hand, truly, I know that her pure and holy story will not be defiled by my impurity; that it will not harm the listener in any way, that my foolishness will not taint it, if he listens to and receives from me this pure, holy, and sweet story that comes from my mouth.

[79]

While I am impure in all my deeds and rotten of character inside and out, I am capable of carrying out useful work just like three other laborers who live in the world. One of them belongs to the pure and two belong to the impure creatures. Even though they are foul, bad, and impure by nature, they please people with their good works. They are the bee, the donkey, and the dog.

The bee belongs to the pure creatures. Yet she is cruel and her poison is bitter. She stings people and causes much pain. However, in her service to human beings, she goes into the wilderness and industriously collects nectar. She also goes down to the stream to draw water and brings it to everything that is important to her work. She is not idle in the least, but ever-diligent. She takes the nectar and puts it into a beehive basket, rock crevice, or tree hollow—wherever she lives. When blessings descend on it from heaven above, then it becomes sweet honeycomb. When someone comes near to her, be it her owner or a stranger, the bee will sting without qualms; she will spare no one.

Those who know her ways will create smoke and fan it in her direction, and she will flee for fear of the smoke. When she withdraws and leaves the honey behind, then they will take it from her. The honey is sweet when eaten, fragrant when smelled, and delights the hearts of kings and lords when made into mead. Furthermore, its wax becomes a lamp for the church and the palace. People do not abandon honey just because of the painful poison of the [80] bee. As for the bee, she is not saddened nor resentful, nor does she abandon working if people take her honey away from her, but rather the next day again goes into the fields as is her habit because she is ordained to be the servant of humanity.

Similarly, I am cruel in my deeds, stinging people with my tongue and causing much pain. However, because I am also ordained to serve you, I have drawn inspiration from the holy books and from the words of the learned fathers and now will write the story of our holy Mother Walatta-Petros, a story that is sweeter than honeycomb and that will delight people's hearts.

As for the donkey, it is impure and yet carries the holy vessels of the house of God, as well as food for the people. Such a holy vessel is not abandoned because of the donkey's impurity; rather, people remove from the donkey what belongs to the house of God and what is needed for sustenance. Similarly, I also carry a chosen vessel and spiritual food: the struggles and virtues of our blessed Mother Walatta-Petros.

The dog is also impure, and yet he goes into the wilderness with his master to hunt. If the dog sees a gazelle or another wild animal, a partridge or other birds that may be eaten, he runs tirelessly to seize it. Then his master pats him, the dog abandons the prey to him, the master takes what has been seized by the dog's mouth, eats it, and does not abandon it just because of the dog's impurity. Similarly, I also hunt in the holy books for the story of the life and [81] holiness of our chosen and beatified Mother Walatta-Petros. I write for you, therefore you should receive this story in faith, like the pure sacrifices, which are the flesh and blood of the Savior during the Eucharist when you say, "Amen and amen"; do not reject it because of my impurity.

Does not the Torah say: Samson found honey in the mouth of a dead lion that he himself had killed earlier? He then ate that honey, and as he himself later put it in a riddle, "From the mouth of the eater came food, from the strong, sweetness." Moreover, when Samson was parched from thirst and near to death, he prayed to God, and God made sweet water flow forth for him from the jawbone of a donkey. Samson then drank and life returned to him, as he himself later put it in a riddle: "A drink in the time of thirst and a weapon for warfare." Also, every day a raven brought food to the prophet Elijah, who took it and ate it and did not consider it impure. If these saints did not deem these impure creatures impure, neither should you deem impure this story that comes from my impure mouth.

[82] As for me, I am not worthy to write this, for I am a sinner and transgressor and because, as it says in the Liturgy, "holy things should be handled by the holy" and "pure things by the pure." Nevertheless, love for Walatta-Petros compelled me to write down for you a few of the many things about her, insofar as allowed by my poor understanding and weak intellect, as well as by what you are able to hear—just like the *dinbeets* bird dives into Lake Tana but can drink only what her tiny stomach allows.

Chapter 2: The Author's Petition

And now you people, lovers of God, who have come from distant regions or who live in this monastery, monks and nuns, fling wide the windows of your ears and awaken your hearts so that you can hear this sweet story I have written down for you. As David says in Psalms, "Hear this, all you peoples, and listen, all who live in the world, in your various lands, you children of Eve, rich and poor! My mouth will speak wisdom, and the meditation of my heart will give counsel. With my ears I will listen to parables, and I will ex-

pound my words with song." He further said, "My people, listen to [83]
my law and incline your ears to the words of my mouth. I will
open my mouth with parables and I will speak in proverbs of old,
all that we have heard and seen, and that our fathers have told us."

Before all else, I thank God who has deemed me worthy of writing this book—I, who have neither worthiness nor ability and am
a fool, the first among fools. It is just as our Lord says in the Gospel, "I trust in you, O Father, and I praise you, Lord of heaven and
earth, who hid this from the wise and the learned and revealed it
to children. Yes, Father, for like this it was your will."

Furthermore, I beg and implore the Lord to help me and grant
to me the power of the word so that I will be able to tell Walatta-
Petros's story from its beginning to its end, lest people mock me
and say, "This man began to build, but then was unable to finish!"
For I am weak of heart and many are those who have wanted to
write these things down but did not because the time and day that
pleased God had not yet come. Indeed, for this reason we of her
community have been distressed for some time that the story of
our holy Mother Walatta-Petros had not been written down for
our benefit, including the virtuous deeds and the miracles that she
performed during her lifetime and after her demise.

Therefore, because spiritual ardor for our holy Mother Walatta-
Petros moved us, we wrote down this book of her *Life and Struggles* in the thirtieth year after she had passed away and found rest, [84]
in 1672–73 CE, in the fifth year of the reign of our King Yohannes,
lover of God, in a year dedicated to Matthew the Evangelist. This
book is to be read out aloud on every November 23, the anniver-
sary of Walatta-Petros's death. May the blessing of her prayers and
the grace of her assistance be with [manuscript owner's name] for
eternity, amen.

Chapter 3: Our Mother's Conception and Birth [85]

Let us begin with the help of God to write the story of the conception and birth of our holy mother of exalted memory, Walatta-
Petros, of a distinguished family and noble lineage, from the house

of Dawaro and Fatagar. Her father's name was Bahir-Saggad, her mother's Kristos-Ebayaa. Both of them were righteous and God-fearing people, as well as very rich in the possessions of this world. People would praise them for all their good deeds, their fasting, prayers, and mercy toward the poor. Her brothers were great lords whose names were Pawlos, Za-Manfas-Qidduus, Lisaana-Kristos, Za-Dinghil, and Yohannes.

As for her father Bahir-Saggad, every year during the August fast of Our Lady Mary's Assumption, he would go to Réma Island in Lake Tana and there fast with a clean heart and a pure mind, out of his love for our Lady Mary. For additional mortification, he would stand in the lake during the night, dressed in a garment of iron, praying and supplicating for the salvation of his soul. When the fasting period was over and the feast of the Assumption arrived, he would prepare a banquet and thereby make the poor and the wretched happy. One day, when he lacked what he needed for the banquet, he became extremely sad, and while he prayed in the lake, as was his custom, he found a fish. When he tore open its belly, in it was gold weighing an ounce. He much marveled at this, rejoicing and praising our Lady Mary. With this gold, he achieved his desire to hold the banquet.

[87]

It was further told about him that while in church during the Liturgy, he would see the mystery of Communion with the host changing from bread to white lamb, and also would see it return to its previous state.

While he was living this kind of life, a righteous monk said to him, "I have seen a great vision, with a bright sun dwelling in the womb of your wife Kristos-Ebayaa."

Bahir-Saggad replied, "Father, please interpret the meaning of your vision to me."

So the monk interpreted the vision to him and said, "A beautiful daughter who will shine like the sun to the ends of the world will be born to you. She will be a guide for the blind of heart, and the kings of the earth and the bishops will bow to her. From the four corners of the world, many people will assemble around her and become one community—people pleasing God. Through her your names Bahir-Saggad and Kristos-Ebayaa will be called out until the consummation of the world."

Bahir-Saggad then also saw a vision like the monk. He told his wife what the righteous monk had imparted to him, and that he himself had seen the same vision. He said to her, "Come, let us hold a vigil and pray with great penitence for seven days so that God may reveal a vision to us and make us certain that this thing is true."

She replied, "Very well." Therefore, that is what they did. After completing a week, he said to her, "Let us do another week since nothing has been revealed to me." Again she said to him, "Very well," and that is what they did. After they had completed the two weeks, they too saw what the righteous monk had seen. However, they kept this thing secret in their hearts until its time had come.

After a few days, Kristos-Ebayaa conceived by the will of God. [89] When the time arrived for her to give birth, pain gripped her. Hearing this, Bahir-Saggad withdrew to a chapel and prayed that she would give birth without pain and suffering. Continuously he sent messengers to the house, one after another. At the proper time, Kristos-Ebayaa gave birth, and a servant who had been sent came carrying the good news and announced to Bahir-Saggad that she had given birth.

He asked, "What is the newborn child, boy or girl?"

The servant responded, "It's a girl."

At that moment, Bahir-Saggad was amazed and praised God because it was fulfilled for him what the righteous monk had told him and what he himself had seen. Therefore, he went happily and exultantly into the house of childbed, even though he was a great lord and it was not appropriate for him to enter into such a house.

They said to him, "How can you enter the house of childbed before the time for entering has arrived?"

Bahir-Saggad responded, "Let me enter, I who already knows! You don't yet know what secret is associated with that girl child." Thus, he entered, sat down, and said to the midwife, "Please show me the child! Give her to me to hold her and kiss her."

The midwife said to him, "How can you hold and kiss a newborn who is all covered in blood?"

He responded, "Give her to me! Truly, there is no unclean blood or filth on this daughter of mine."

Therefore, the midwife wrapped her in a garment of fine linen and gave her to him. He received her and carried her in his arms for a while, looking her in the face and kissing her head. He marveled at the beauty of her appearance and said to her, "You are blessed, child that God has chosen and sanctified to be his servant while still in your mother's womb!" Having said this, Bahir-Saggad left the room and went away.

On account of all this, we consider blessed Walatta-Petros's father and mother who brought forth for us this blessed and holy mother through whom we have found salvation. She became our guide toward righteousness and hope, she revealed to us the way [90] of renunciation and of monastic life, and taught us the law of love and humility. If they had not brought her forth for us, our lives would have been destined for perdition. As the prophet Isaiah says in the Bible, "If the Lord of Hosts had not left us a seed, we would have become like Sodom and would have resembled Gomorrah." Behold, in her the sign of her parents' righteousness was visible, since the good tree produces good fruit, but the bad tree produces bad fruit. As our Lord says in the Gospel, "No good tree produces bad fruit, and no bad tree produces good fruit. Every tree is known by its fruit." Saint Paul further says in the Bible, "If the first fruit is holy, the entire dough also will be holy, and if the root is holy, the branches also will be holy."

Chapter 4: Our Mother's Baptism and Childhood

When the infant was eighty days old, they baptized her in Christian baptism according to the order of the *Book of Baptism* and named her Walatta-Petros. And truly, she was a daughter of Saint Peter, since the work of the father is found in the one who is born from him. As our Lord said to Peter, "Upon you I will build my church," and upon her, too, the Lord built a community and made them a house of God. As Paul says, "You all are the house of the Lord." Just as the Lord gave Peter the keys to the Kingdom of Heaven, so he likewise gave to Walatta-Petros that those who follow her will enter into the Kingdom of Heaven. And as the Lord said three times to Peter, "Tend my sheep," so to her likewise he conferred the tending of his sheep in the pasture of meritorious spiritual struggle.

She truly was worthy of this name of Walatta-Petros since the son of a king becomes a king and the son of a priest becomes a priest; and just as Peter became the head of the apostles, she likewise became the head of all religious teachers. Just as Peter could [91] kill and resurrect through his authority, she likewise could kill and resurrect. She became a god by grace, as scripture says, "You are gods, all of you are children of the Most High." O glory, glory of such dimensions! O sublimity, sublimity of such greatness! While she was a human being like us, to her it was given to be a god.

But let us return to our story. The young girl was pleasant to look at and had a beautiful figure. The look in her eyes was like a shining star; her teeth were white like milk. As Solomon says in the Song of Songs, "You are wholly beautiful; there is no flaw in you. There is nothing ugly upon you." But the outer beauty of her appearance was surpassed by the inner beauty of her mind. Listen, my loved ones: What should make us boastful of the beauty of our appearance, which changes and decays? Is a human being justified before God by his beautiful appearance, or damned by his ugly aspect?

About this the Torah says, Rachel had a beautiful appearance and beautiful eyes, and Jacob loved her very much. For seven years he served her father for the sake of her. Yet her father did not give her to him, but stealthily gave him Leah; and Leah, instead, had bleary eyes and Jacob did not love her. As soon as he saw her, he was very distressed. However, Laban, the girls' father, said to him, "Do not be in pain. This doesn't happen in our country; people do not first give the younger one while an older unmarried one is there. Complete another seven years of service, and I will give her to you, too." So Jacob again served Laban for seven years, and Laban then gave Rachel to him, too.

God, by contrast, favored Leah—who was despised because she was ugly in appearance and had bleary eyes—by opening her womb, and so she gave birth to Judah from whose seed Christ was [92] born. As Jacob said, "Kingship will not vanish from Judah, nor princely power from his member." As for Rachel, who had beautiful eyes and whom Jacob loved, God did not love her and did not give her a child, so ultimately she became jealous of her sister. So she said to Jacob, "Give me a child, or else I will die!" With great difficulty Rachel then gave birth to Joseph and to Benjamin, but from their seed Christ was not born. God for his part does not look at outer beauty but at inner beauty.

Furthermore, the Torah says: Esau was beautiful in his appearance and Isaac loved him, while Jacob was ugly in his appearance and God loved him. He says, "Jacob I loved, but Esau I hated." Also, Christ was not born from the seed of Esau but from that of Jacob. David, too, says in Psalms, "He took me from my father's sheep and anointed me with holy oil. My brothers were handsome and older, but God was not pleased with them." Because of this, we should not boast about the beauty of our looks, nor need we be ashamed of the ugliness of our appearance, since that which is perishable should clothe itself with that which is imperishable.

Listen further and we will tell you more of the story of Bahir-Saggad, the father of our holy Mother Walatta-Petros. He loved her more than all his grown male children, with his whole heart and his entire mind, and he was proud of her. While she was still a child and of a tender age so that she did not yet know her father's and mother's name, he used to put her on a chair and on a bed. He would take his sword and pace in front of her, lifting up his feet and marching for her, just like soldiers march in front of the king. He would sing her name and say to her, "I will die for you, I, your father, blessed child whom God has chosen, blessed and made holy." He would do this every day, not only after having had his fill and being drunk but while he was hungry and thirsty. Truly, he
[93]

was drunk with love for her and knew the secret of what would happen through her.

Nevertheless, he soon died and his joy did not have fulfillment. He desired but did not see, he looked but did not find. As our Lord says in the Gospel, "Truly, many prophets and righteous ones wanted to see what you see but did not see it."

Chapter 5: Our Mother's Marriage and Children

Therefore, her mother and brothers then raised our holy Mother Walatta-Petros, in wisdom and the fear of God, and taught her the books of the Church. When she grew up and reached the legal age for marriage, they gave her to one of the great lords of the land whose name was Malkiya-Kristos—he was the chief adviser of King Susinyos, who sat on the throne having adopted the faith of the Europeans—so that she would become his wife, according to the ritual of matrimony for the daughters of great lords, in order to procreate. For scripture says, "Be many and multiply and fill the earth." When Malkiya-Kristos brought her into his house, he loved her very much; he knew her, and she conceived.

She then, like Martha, prayed to God, using these words: "If this unborn child that is inside my womb shall be born and please you, may it live; but if not, may it quickly die." When her pregnancy [94] reached term she gave birth. She had the boy child baptized, but then he immediately died, God having listened to her prayer. Saying the same prayer, she gave birth to three children, and all of them died by the will of God. Nonetheless, Malkiya-Kristos, the husband of our holy Mother Walatta-Petros, was very generous and still loved her very much. Yet she did not want to stay with him because she now bore in mind the transience of the world.

As the Apostle Peter says in the Bible, "All flesh is like grass, and all the glory of man is like the flower of the grass." And John the Evangelist further says, "Do not love the world and that which is in the world because everything in the world is the desire of the eye and the desire of the flesh. Life's distress does not come from the Father but from the world. In addition, the world will perish, and its desires will perish." Moreover, Paul says, "It is right, O our brothers, that it be like this, because all the things of this world are soon to perish: Those people who have married shall be as if they did not marry, those who live comfortably as if they did not live comfortably, those who cry as if they did not cry, those who rejoice as if they did not rejoice, those who purchase as if they did not purchase, those who have possessions as if they did not have them, those who eat as if they did not eat, and those who drink as if they did not drink, since all the pleasures of this world will pass and perish." Furthermore, our Lord says in the Gospel, "What would it benefit man if he gained the entire world but lost his soul? What can man give as ransom for his soul?"

[95]   This is why our holy Mother Walatta-Petros spent all her days in fasting and prayer, while in the evenings she entered into the church and kept vigil all night without interruption, in turns standing upright and prostrating herself as well as praying in all manners. Thus, she would go into ecstasy and disappear from the view of the women who had followed her. At dawn, she would reappear to them and return home.

Every Sunday Walatta-Petros would sponsor a meal for the clergy of the church. With her was a woman who cooked the stews and the other various dishes. That woman used to grumble; she did not like to cook for the clergy. When our holy Mother Walatta-Petros understood what that woman harbored in her mind, one evening she took the woman with her to the church and let her see the vigil and exertions of the clergy.

As a result, the woman repented and said, "I have sinned! Forgive me for causing you distress. Before this, I didn't know what the priests did, but now I have seen it and marveled at them. From now on I will certainly do all you desire and will not disobey your orders."

Those who know Walatta-Petros's story further relate: When our holy Mother Walatta-Petros celebrated a holiday with a banquet, she provided everything the body needs, all kinds of food and drink, as well as meats. She then assembled the poor and wretched, all the people of the town as well as the priests of the church, and seated them at the table, each one at the seat that was due to them. Then they would eat and drink until they had had enough and were happy. She, on the other hand, would not taste anything from all this but would eat cooked bitter leaves and drink only water, [96] while it appeared to the others that she ate and drank like them. Nobody from among the people at the banquet knew this about her except for the maidservant who served her. For a long time she maintained this way of life, and desired not at all the pleasures of this ephemeral world.

She lived a regular married life with her husband Malkiya-Kristos but waited and looked for the day on which it would please God for her to leave, escaping and fleeing from her husband, abandoning the world and becoming a nun. She prayed continuously for this and implored God, saying, "Show me your way, Lord, and teach me your path. Lead me with your righteousness, and, O Lord, teach me, your servant, your path, the right path." Our holy Mother Walatta-Petros kept praying like this.

Chapter 6: Our Mother Tries to Take Up the Holy Life

When the time came that it pleased God for her to leave this worldly life, her husband Malkiya-Kristos went on a military campaign with the king. As for her, she stayed in the region of Simaada, on the third story of the couple's castle where no one could see her. At that time, by the will of God, two monks came to our holy Mother Walatta-Petros, Father Yamaana-Kristos of Réma Island Monastery and Father Tazkaara-Dinghil of Tsana Island Monastery. They had been sent by Father Fatla-Sillasé to bring her stealthily out of her husband's home and take her with them to the Zagé peninsula, in southwest Lake Tana. When she saw them, she was very happy. In charity, she then gave all her possessions to the [97] poor and the wretched. In addition, she took all her jewelry, eighty ounces weight of gold, in order to distribute it to the needy and to churches on their way. They then came to an agreement about the time when they would leave. When it became evening and after people had fallen asleep, she summoned her three maidservants,

Maryamaweet, Eskindiraweet, and Iyopraxia, so that they would follow her.

Then our holy Mother Walatta-Petros left the castle, and the monks received her, took her with them, and made her mount a mule. They spent the entire night walking and thus in only one day reached the Abode of Our Lady Mary Church at Racha; there they rested. Then she began to distribute the gold all along the way. What is truly astonishing and wondrous, though, is that within just one day she marched such a long way, even though she was weak and her body tender. If it had not been for the power of God that strengthened her, who would have been able to march like that? Not even a strong young man could have marched like that, let alone a woman like her. For she lacked strength and her feet were delicate because she had never trod the earth before in her entire life. If she got up from her resting couch, she would stand upon a carpet that had been spread out, and if so much as fallen dry breadcrumbs found her there, they hurt her feet so that they would bleed. However, the power of God strengthened her, and she did not feel any weakness because she was inebriated with love for him. She was drawn to her destination like someone invited to a wedding or like a mighty warrior to a prize. And indeed, our holy Mother Walatta-Petros marched to a heavenly wedding and to the groom Jesus Christ; indeed, she marched toward a prize, fighting against the devil and taking from him many souls that he had made his prey.

[98] Again they set off from Racha and came to Chegwaré-Zigba town, and then, moving on from there, to Wonchet town. There they hid in the house of an old nun named Amata-Petros; she remained there for a few days. Then our holy Mother Walatta-Petros set off from Wonchet, went to Robeet town, and eventually reached Emabra town opposite the Zagé peninsula on Lake Tana. There, at the lakeshore, was a man named Kifla-Maryam, who owned a boat and was a good person. Thus, Walatta-Petros became his guest: he received her, took her into his house, and gave her shelter. The next day he came with the boat and took her to the monastic settlement of Zagé. When she arrived there, she was happy and gave

thanks to the Lord. She greeted the saints who lived in that monastic settlement, monks and nuns, and implored them to kindly
remember her in their prayers.

Then she remained there, saying, "This is my resting place forever. Here I will live because I have chosen it." She therefore shaved
her head's hair and put on a nun's cap.

Chapter 7: Our Mother's Husband Hunts Her Down [101]

When her husband, Malkiya-Kristos, while he was at the camp
with the king, learned that our holy Mother Walatta-Petros had
fled and disappeared, he told the king and asked leave so that he
could go tracking her and searching for her. The king gave him
permission and dispatched him. Malkiya-Kristos set out immediately, in great anger and roaring like a lion.

He called up his regiment, named Siltaan Marid, which he had
set up in the region of Wuddo, along with their leader, a colonel.
He took them with him and crisscrossed the entire region, asking
around about where Walatta-Petros had gone, and people told him
that she had entered Zagé Monastery. Straightaway, he surrounded
the town of Robeet and ordered his regiment Siltaan Marid to destroy it, plunder the inhabitants' possessions, eat up their provisions without restraint, and have no mercy. When they found that
man Kifla-Maryam, the owner of the boat, they took him prisoner,
plundered his goods, and seized his livestock. They acted according to Malkiya-Kristos's orders.

The people of the town, men and women, broke out in cries of
wailing, and there was great upheaval.

Malkiya-Kristos furthermore told the soldiers' leader, "Build a
lookout in a treetop at the lakeshore, climb up it, observe the boats
that come and go in each direction, and if you discover Walatta-
Petros, arrest her." That man did as his lord had ordered him,
climbing up to the lookout and keeping watch day and night.
Whenever he saw a boat coming, he went down to look at it, and
if she was not in it, he let it go.

[102]   On his part, Malkiya-Kristos had gone to Woynayat town to Lady Walatta-Giyorgis, daughter of the late king Sartsa-Dinghil, and to Father Fatla-Sillasé.

They rebuked him, saying to him, "Why did you lay waste to the town of Robeet without reason and bring ruin to people who did nothing wrong or unjust? Beware of God's wrath coming down upon you!"

Immediately, he fell at their feet and replied, "I entrust myself to you; pass judgment on me and bring about peace between me and my wife. If I have done anything wrong against her in the past, she shall have her compensation. From now on, though, I will not commit any wrongdoing again. Even if she tells me, 'Quit being a soldier of the king!,' I will quit it for her sake, as she has chosen." While he spoke these things, he cried and spilled tears.

After they had heard his words, they said to him, "These words of yours are not sincere. Rather, they will change tomorrow." So he swore a strict oath before them.

Following this, Father Fatla-Sillasé went to our holy Mother Walatta-Petros and told her about the devastation of the town of Robeet that had come about because of her, and about all that Malkiya-Kristos had spoken, and that he had sworn a strict oath.

After our holy Mother Walatta-Petros had heard this, she said, "No! No! I will not leave this monastic settlement, and neither will I reconcile with him."

Father Fatla-Sillasé rebuked her, telling her, "If it is you who leave him, and if he marries another woman, his transgression is your fault. As for me, I advise you that reconciling with him is [103]   better for you. If he has acted wrongfully against you in the past, take your compensation. Concerning the future, I have made him swear that he will not wrong you again. Furthermore, since the people of the town of Robeet wept because of the devastation they suffered, God is displeased with you. He does not love your repudiation of the world and will not accept your prayers."

Our holy Mother Walatta-Petros responded with these words, "I know Malkiya-Kristos's character, that it is not founded on righteousness. However, I will obey your word, my father and teacher. It shall be as you said so that the people of the town of Robeet will not complain about me. You have to swear to me, though, that you will not make me see the face of his mother."

He replied, "Very well," and they agreed on this. Father Fatla-Sillasé then left first, in order to send her a mule, while our holy Mother Walatta-Petros remained there for the night.

Do you see, my loved ones, the noble virtue of our holy Mother Walatta-Petros, in that she returned herself to Malkiya-Kristos, saying, "I prefer that I should perish rather than all the people perish on account of me"? This is reminiscent of what our Lord said to the guards who came to arrest him. As the Gospel says, "The Lord Jesus said to them, 'Who are you looking for?' and they replied, 'Jesus of Nazareth.' He responded, 'I am he. If you want me, let these disciples go.'" Our holy Mother Walatta-Petros did likewise and said, "God's will be done! He can save me; to him nothing is impossible. He who saved Sarah from the hands of Pharaoh, the king of Egypt, and from the hands of Abimelech, king of Gerara, he will also save me. He who saved Susanna from the hands of the old men, he will also save me. He who saved my abducted country- [104] woman Egzi-Harayaa from the hands of the evil king Motalami, he will also save me."

In addition, she said, "'I do not fear evil because you, Lord, are with me.' 'God will shine a light for me and will save me; what then can make me afraid? God is my life's refuge; what then can terrify me?' 'I put my trust in God; I have nothing to fear. What can men do to me?'" Raising this and similar prayers, she spent the entire night.

Chapter 8: Our Mother Returns to Her Husband

The next night they put a boat in water and had our Mother Walatta-Petros and her maidservants get in it. The boatmen were Father Yamaana-Kristos and Father Tazkaara-Dinghil; they poled it, one at the prow and the other at the stern.

While they were on the open water, the soldiers who were watching for them from on high in the lookout heard their voices and recognized them from their words, since the clerical boatmen abused Malkiya-Kristos and reviled his mother. Our holy Mother Walatta-Petros, however, reprimanded them, saying, "Why do you talk so much and heap scorn on a noblewoman? Do your mouths have no locks?"

After the soldiers had climbed down from the lookout and hid themselves from Walatta-Petros's party, some of them ran to their lord to tell him the good news. The voyagers, for their part, reached the lakeshore at Emabra and docked their boat. Since it was night and morning had not yet come, they did not see the soldiers who had hid themselves from them and lay in wait for them. Walatta-Petros and her companions remained on the lakeshore until morning came and until Walatta-Petros would be sent a mule.

[105]   As soon as morning had come, the commander of the soldiers emerged from where he had hidden and wanted to arrest the monks. When they resisted him, he got rough with them and abused them, saying, "You are rascally monks who do violence to a married woman! Today, though, God has abandoned you and given you into my hands." He then held his sword sideways, inside its sheath, and struck them in order to frighten them. The commander hit Father Tazkaara-Dinghil's legs and wounded him; the scar from the wound remained on his legs until he died.

Immediately, our holy Mother Walatta-Petros rose up in great anger, slapped the commander on his cheeks, and said to him, "You insolent servant, how dare you disrespect me!"

Those other soldiers reached Malkiya-Kristos and informed him about finding Walatta-Petros. When he heard this news he rose up with joy, mounted his horse, and hurried to her. He forgot his oath and wanted to seize her and take her away, without Father Fatla-Sillasé and Lady Walatta-Giyorgis knowing.

He knocked her nun's cap off her head, prodded her from behind with his feet, and said to her, "Get going!"

Upon that, our holy Mother Walatta-Petros immediately let herself fall on the ground and acted as if dead. She kept silent and obstinately stopped moving. It was not possible to put her on a mule. Malkiya-Kristos then ordered his soldiers to transport her by grasping her wrists and ankles through her clothes. However, they almost were unable to move her. With great difficulty they carried her a short distance. Everywhere on their way there were thorns, and walking was difficult for them. Therefore, they set her on the ground. As for Malkiya-Kristos, he became enraged, gnashing his teeth, frightening the soldiers, and scowling at them.

At that time, the soldiers began to implore Walatta-Petros with gentle words, saying, "Our merciful and compassionate lady, have mercy on us and be kind to us, as is your custom! For if you resist us and we are unable to carry you therefore, our lord will get angry with us and will kill us. Comply with us and show us compassion." When she heard their words, she had mercy on them and stood up so they could put her on a mule. [106]

While they said these things, there arrived envoys who had been sent by Father Fatla-Sillasé and Lady Walatta-Giyorgis. These envoys said to Malkiya-Kristos, "How could you lie to us, deceive us, and secretly, unknown to us, go and seize her on the road like a thief and bandit? You made a childish judgment! This decision of yours is not going to be a good one. Now we are telling you to come here, to our home at Woynayat, and she shall come too, so that we can effect a reconciliation between you. If, however, you refuse to come, being contemptuous of us and not heeding our word, we will consider ourselves wronged by you, and together with us God will have been wronged."

When Malkiya-Kristos heard this message, he became afraid, changed his mind, and set off toward them. As for our holy Mother Walatta-Petros, they made her mount a mule and conveyed her to them at Woynayat, too. There, Father Fatla-Sillasé and Lady Walatta-Giyorgis adjudicated between them, reconciled them, and dispatched them in peace. Thus, our holy Mother Walatta-Petros and Malkiya-Kristos returned to their region of Simaada.

Chapter 9: Our Mother Leaves Her Husband Again

After this, our holy Mother Walatta-Petros lived looking for a reason to separate from Malkiya-Kristos. In those days, the faith of the Europeans had begun in Ethiopia and our Father Simeon, the patriarch of the Orthodox Church, had been killed, along with the anti-Catholic rebel Yolyos, so that they became martyrs. That man, the patriarch's killer, then took the patriarch's vestment and gave it to Malkiya-Kristos. When our holy Mother Walatta-Petros learned about this, her mind shuddered and she was filled with revulsion for Malkiya-Kristos. She refused to come close to him and stopped sleeping with him.

[107]

She said to him, "How can I live with you when you are not a Christian? You have had the patriarch killed! And look: You have the patriarch's vestment in your possession!"

After this, she ceased eating and drinking, and abandoned beautifying herself in the manner of women. She did not style her hair or put on oils and perfumes, nor perfume herself by burning various fragrant substances, nor paint her fingernails, nor color her eyelids with kohl, nor adorn herself with beautiful clothes. She gave up all these things, as well as other similar ones. She lived like a nun, making herself wretched in every way.

When Malkiya-Kristos saw our holy Mother Walatta-Petros's behavior and the determination of her heart, and when furthermore it pleased God, he said to her on his own account, without anybody forcing him, "For how long will you live with me like this? Go where you please: I will not hinder you."

She replied, "Swear to me that you will not go back on your word."

So he swore to her. He also asked her likewise. So she swore to him.

The next day she said to him, "Dispatch me according to your word."

He replied, "Very well," and ordered his soldiers to saddle a mule, make her mount it, and accompany her.

[108]

He also sent word to her family, "Take back your daughter. After I reconciled with her, she never made me happy but only gave me displeasure. In addition, she is no longer one body with me as is the decree for husband and wife. From now on, she may do as she wants and pleases."

At that time all the people of his household, men and women, wailed and cried and said to their lord, "Don't let her go!"

He replied, "But I have sworn an oath and therefore it is impossible for me to hold her back." It was not he who let her go, however, but rather the will of God that prevented him from reneging.

Then our holy Mother Walatta-Petros mounted a mule and went on her way, with crying and wailing men and women seeing her off because she was leaving them. In sadness they returned to their homes. Those others who had been dispatched together with her took her to her brother Za-Dinghil, told him about their mission, and then returned home. Za-Dinghil received her well and accommodated her in his residence.

As for Walatta-Petros, she was very happy and glad. She praised God, saying, "I would rather be a castaway in the house of God than live pleasantly in the house of sinners."

When our holy Mother Walatta-Petros had left her home, she had not taken anything with her, neither gold nor silver to sustain her on the way, nor a staff, nor shoes, even though she was the wife of a lord and the daughter of noble parents. As our Lord said to the disciples, "Acquire for yourselves neither gold nor silver." Rather, she had left her husband's home with nothing, saying, like Job in the Bible, "Naked did I emerge from my mother's womb, and naked will I return to the womb of the grave."

As David says in Psalms, "The law from your mouth is better for me than countless amounts of gold and silver." "This is why I have loved your commandment more than gold and topaz." What, then, is God's commandment? Is it not to renounce possessions and to carry the cross? Our Lord further says, "It is easier for a camel to pass through the eye of a needle than for a rich man to enter into the Kingdom of Heaven." In addition, the *Sayings of the Fathers* relate, "Dear ones, what is gold? Is it not an evil shackle and a chain? Iron only destroys the body, while gold is an affliction for the body and a torment for the soul." And again Paul says, "The love of money is the root of all evil" because through it many went astray and deserted their faith. This is why our holy Mother Walatta-Petros also abhorred worldly wealth and regarded it as nothing. [109]

Chapter 10: Our Mother Leaves Her
Brother's House to Become a Nun

A short time thereafter, when our holy Mother Walatta-Petros had made up her mind to go away and become a nun, she said to her brother Za-Dinghil, "Allow me to go visit my spiritual teacher Father Fatla-Sillasé because he is sick and suffers. It has been a long time since I have seen him. If he dies without me seeing him, he will curse me. Truly, the spiritual father is greater than the corporeal father."

Za-Dinghil replied, "Go ahead," not realizing that she had spoken to him deceptively and with cunning words; she appeared sincere to him. Thus, he ordered his retainers to saddle a mule for her, help her to mount it, guard her on the way, and conduct her to her teacher. They acted on her behalf as her brother had ordered them. Thus, she went, while with her were her maidservants, who always followed her.

When she was close to reaching the town of Robeet, she told the retainers, "Help me dismount. I will camp here today. I don't want to increase the burden on my teacher since we are many and he cannot host all of us. So, you, return on your way. You can collect me again another day because I will remain with my teacher quite a while." With these words, she sent them away, and they went.

She had already premeditated this decision with her teacher. He had devised this ruse craftily so that they would not feel betrayed by or hostile toward him. Thus, our holy Mother Walatta-Petros stayed behind, together with her maidservants.

[111]   She proceeded to the house of one of the people of a nearby town and spent the night there. However, when it was deep night and all the maidservants were asleep, she woke up a young servant girl to guide her to her teacher's house. Together with that girl, she then stealthily left, walking on foot, while her blood flowed like water because the sharp edges of the stones cut into her feet. They were truly soft, like the feet of an infant just come from its moth-

er's womb. The people who saw that blood the next morning wondered among themselves:

"What is this blood? Is it the blood of a goat or a sheep that a leopard has torn apart, or that a thief has slaughtered?"

On her part, our holy Mother Walatta-Petros, proceeding slowly together with the girl, reached the town of Robeet the next day and entered into the Presentation of Our Lady Mary Church, its sanctuary. She sat down in the church courtyard of the people of that place.

They, however, said to her, "Get up! We don't have a lodging place here. Rather, go into the town where you will find lodging."

She replied, "I will not go to the town but will stay in your courtyard." Then, when evening came, they allowed her into a hut that a nun had abandoned. For that week, our holy Mother Walatta-Petros went and lived there, together with that girl. She came to like that hut very much and wanted to stay there until God's judgment.

Chapter 11: Our Mother Finds a New Servant

That girl gave her much trouble, however, more than that of one hundred people. So Walatta-Petros became very distressed and said to herself, "If I found someone who, for my benefit, would take her with them, I would send her back. I would prefer to remain behind on my own in order to find rest from trouble and live in tranquility." [112]

When God saw the strength of her distress, he brought a woman to Walatta-Petros who was going to that town from which the girl originated. So our holy Mother Walatta-Petros asked that woman to take the girl back to her home and dispatched her with the girl. Our holy Mother Walatta-Petros then remained behind alone. However, God did not abandon her.

On that very day, a young servant woman came to her who had been sent by Lebaseeta-Kristos, who was living in Furé. Because she had heard the news about our holy Mother Walatta-Petros, Lebaseeta-Kristos had sent the young woman in order to pay our holy Mother Walatta-Petros a visit and investigate her situation. The young woman arrived alone among the other passersby, came near to that place where Walatta-Petros stayed, and inquired, "Where does the lady stranger live?"

She came to Walatta-Petros's hut without anybody guiding her. She stood at the gate and clapped her hands, as is the custom in monasteries. So our holy Mother Walatta-Petros stuck her head out of the door, looked at the young woman, and with her hands beckoned her since she was alone that day, without anybody serving her. The young woman then approached her, and our holy Mother Walatta-Petros asked her, "Where are you from? And for whom have you come?"

The young woman replied, "My mistress Lebaseeta-Kristos has sent me to you. She says to you, 'How are you? And, how are you doing? Peace be unto you, and may the peace of God be with you, amen.'"

When our holy Mother Walatta-Petros heard this salutation, she was amazed and praised God who had not let her live alone for a single day. So the young woman stayed with her for that day.

The next day, however, she said to Walatta-Petros, "Allow me to go to my mistress and bring her your return message."

But our holy Mother Walatta-Petros replied, "Stay with me this week because I am alone."

[113] The young woman answered, "Very well." Truly, she was of good character; she spoke with ease, and appropriately, and was loved by all. She stayed with Walatta-Petros and pleased her doubly since, before, Walatta-Petros had been distressed on account of the spiteful deeds of that girl who had gone away.

Do you see the justness of God's understanding? He chased away the young servant girl who had accompanied Walatta-Petros into exile but drew close this young servant woman who had been far away, and made her stay with Walatta-Petros. He truly is all-powerful. He acts as he pleases and what he decides he carries out. Nobody can argue with him. He removes what is nearby and brings close what is distant. Truly, he scrutinizes the heart and the kidneys.

Chapter 12: Our Mother Meets Her Lifelong Companion Eheta-Kristos

In those days, while our holy Mother Walatta-Petros was living with that young woman, Father Tsigé-Haymanot came from Furé to visit her when he heard the news that she was in Robeet. When he arrived there, he met with her and learned that she lived alone. He said to her, "My child, how can you live alone without a companion? This is not good for you."

Our holy Mother Walatta-Petros replied, "How do I do that? From where can I find a companion who will live with me? Am I not a stranger in this town?"

He responded, "If you want, I myself will bring you one. There is a fine woman named Eheta-Kristos who, like you, left her husband and home, became a nun, and now lives with her sister. This would be good for both of you."

Our holy Mother Walatta-Petros replied, "As for me, I don't want to live with a woman who has left her home." [114]

He responded, "But, I know that woman's character: it is good. If you see her yourself, you will like her."

Having said this, he took leave from her and returned to Furé. There he then said to Eheta-Kristos, "If you live a pampered life with your sister, and fatten your body with food and drink, how have you repudiated the world? And which pleasure have you ever abandoned for the sake of God? Truly, it would have been better for you to stay in your home with your husband than to live your current life! However, if you listen to my word and accept my pronouncement, I advise you as follows: It would be better for you to live together with Walatta-Petros who is at Robeet. She truly is a fine woman." Then he revealed to her all that Walatta-Petros had done, from the beginning to the end.

Eheta-Kristos replied, "But I don't want to live with a woman who has lived at court! If I were to live with her, what might she teach me, and what example might I take from her? Both of us are indeed new plants in the religious life."

He replied, "Please go to meet her once to observe her character and examine her conduct. If you like her, you can stay with her, but if you dislike her, nobody will force you to live with her."

Eheta-Kristos said to him, "Very well. I will do this so that your will may be done. However, I absolutely don't want to live with her."

Then Eheta-Kristos secretly went to our holy Mother Walatta-Petros in a boat, without anyone knowing about it except the two of them, namely, Eheta-Kristos and Father Tsigé-Haymanot. She arrived at the place, stood at the gate, and clapped her hands. So our holy Mother Walatta-Petros said to the young servant woman who now served her, "Go out, please, and inquire who is clapping."

When the young woman came out, she recognized Eheta-Kristos. She returned and told our holy Mother Walatta-Petros that [115] it was Eheta-Kristos because she knew her from before, when she had been at Furé. Our holy Mother Walatta-Petros said to her, "Tell her 'Come in!' " So the maidservant went and brought Eheta-Kristos in.

As soon as our holy Mother Walatta-Petros and Eheta-Kristos saw each other from afar, love was infused into both their hearts, love for each other, and, approaching, they exchanged the kiss of greeting. Then they sat down and told each other stories about the workings of God. There was no fear or mistrust between them. They were like people who had known each other beforehand because the Holy Spirit united them.

Chapter 13: Our Mother and Eheta-Kristos Decide to Live Together and Become Nuns

They then deliberated together and decided that they would live together. So Eheta-Kristos said to Walatta-Petros, "I will now return to Furé and send you a boat, so you can come there. Then we will meet to ponder the plan that God has revealed to us." Immediately, Eheta-Kristos went and sent her the boat. Our holy Mother

Walatta-Petros received it and arrived at Furé. There she greeted
Father Tsigé-Haymanot and all the devout sisters who were there.
Then Eheta-Kristos came and greeted her like a stranger whom she
had not known before.

Thereafter Father Tsigé-Haymanot said to the two of them,
when they were alone, "My daughters, how have you fared? Did
you take a liking to each other or not?"

They replied, "We love each other very much indeed. However,
we do not know how to flee and escape our families."

He responded, "Indeed, this is also a challenge for me." He then
said to Eheta-Kristos, "You tell your sister, 'I do not enjoy living
with you in comfort and abundance. It doesn't seem a righteous
thing to me. Therefore, with your permission, allow me to become
a disciple of the pious nun Ersinna. If not, I will run away from you
and go to where you will never see me again.'"

They said to him, "What you say is good. However, you yourself
should go to Eheta-Kristos's sister and get this done."

So he went and told this to Eheta-Kristos's sister. In response,
she said to him, "Very well. Let it be as you said. I herewith give
her permission to leave."

Father Tsigé-Haymanot then took Walatta-Petros to Ersinna   [116]
and revealed his secret plan to the latter, adding, "Don't reveal this
secret to anyone." He then got a boat ready for Walatta-Petros and
Eheta-Kristos and by night dispatched them, telling them, "Today
go back to Zagé and stay there for three days so that those who
are after you will not find you." They did as he had instructed them.

Three days later, Walatta-Petros and Eheta-Kristos climbed
aboard that same boat and went to Robeet, where our holy Mother
Walatta-Petros had lived before, and there lived together in mutual
love, like soul and body. From that day onward, the two did not
separate, neither in times of tribulation and persecution nor in
those of tranquility, but only in death.

After some days, they went to Dabra Anqo Monastery, and
there our holy Mother Walatta-Petros took on the habit and dedicated herself devotedly to the service of God, with fasts and
prayers and all kinds of virtuous deeds. She also began the labor

of humility and took up menial work like a maidservant. Thus, in a single day she would grind five measures of barley or of wheat, even though her hands were delicate and not used to grinding or to any work at all.

With her were Eheta-Kristos and Walatta-Pawlos, daughter of Duke Atinatewos. Their meeting and living together there was a fine thing, just as David says in Psalms, "Mercy and justice have met, righteousness and peace have kissed." "It is good and pleasant indeed when sisters are together."

[118]

As for our holy Mother Walatta-Petros, nobody resembled or equaled her in all kinds of work. If she occupied herself with the preparation of the stew, it turned out tasty and delicious smelling, and so abundant that it exceeded the measure. Or if she went out into the countryside in order to collect firewood, a large load immediately came together for her. In all she did, God gave her success. Furthermore, she used to go to a faraway river carrying a jar. There she would draw water and carry it back. To do so, she had to climb up a steep ascent on all fours. On that path, there was a large stone where she used to sit down and rest a bit, catching her breath, because her body was exhausted. People call this stone "Walatta-Petros's Resting Place," and even today everybody who goes up or down this ascent kisses and salutes it. It will remain a monument to the memory of her name until the consummation of the world. From there, she would then rise up again, carrying that jar and returning to their home. Everybody who saw her marveled. Walking the length of the path to that river took from dawn to 9:00 a.m.

The sisters who were with her did likewise because she was their example and she taught them the works of humility. As our Lord says, "He who among you wants to be a leader should be a servant to the others." Similarly, the Apostle Peter says, "Be examples for his flock, so that when the Lord of the shepherds appears, you may obtain the crown of glory that does not wither."

In the monastery there also were idle and lazy nuns who did no work at all and lived in sloth. They let their fingernails grow and beautified themselves. Yet when they saw the humility and toil of our holy Mother Walatta-Petros, they began to scold and rebuke

[119]

themselves, saying, "Woe and doubly woe are we who have spent our days in laziness and indolence, even though we are poor people's daughters and the wives of Walatta-Petros's servants and retainers. Normally we would be grinding grain and fetching water. We have not been mindful of the day of our death and have ignored that there will be a retribution for the lazy. Yet, Walatta-Petros—a lady, a daughter of nobles, and the wife of a lord—has made herself poor and entered through the narrow gate that leads to eternal life. By contrast, we are in the broad gate that leads to perdition." Having considered this, they repented of their past behavior, emulated our holy Mother Walatta-Petros, and began to work like her.

Of how many virtuous deeds of our holy Mother Walatta-Petros could we tell? They are oh so many! Moreover, the prayers, prostrations, and virtuous deeds that she performed secretly remain unknown: the works of the righteous are concealed.

Chapter 14: King Susinyos Establishes the Filthy Faith of the Europeans

After this, King Susinyos began to make changes and established the filthy faith of the Europeans, Catholicism, which says: Christ has two natures, even after he, in his divine and human natures, became one and he became the perfect human being. Thereby, Susinyos repudiated the holy faith of Alexandria, which says as [120] follows: Christ became the perfect human being; he is not split or divided in anything he does; he is one Son. In him there is only one aspect, one essence, and one divine nature, namely, that of God the Logos.

When our holy Mother Walatta-Petros heard this, she could not bear it but withdrew and fled from place to place, exiling herself until she reached Tsiyaat together with her female companions, whom we mentioned before.

As the Gospel says, "Blessed are those who are persecuted for the sake of righteousness because they will have the Kingdom of

Heaven." It further says, "Turn away from the lying prophets who come to you in sheep's clothing while inside they are ravenous wolves. By their fruits you shall know them." In addition, Paul says, "Our brothers, I implore you to beware of those who create turmoil and bring quarrels against the doctrine you have learned. Truly, they serve their belly and not God, and with artful language and pleasant manners lead astray many simple people." Do not waver and "do not place yourselves under the yoke of the unbelievers." Therefore, leave their midst and separate from them. God says, "Do not come close to the impure. I will receive you and be your father, and you will be my sons and daughters." Thus says God, who has power over everything. Furthermore, the *Rules for the Monks* says, "Do not pray together with *arseesaan*, that is to say, heretics."

[121]

This is why our holy Mother Walatta-Petros kept away from them and fled, going to the faraway region of Tsiyaat so as not to hear the blasphemy of the Europeans and not to have company with anyone who had joined that creed.

There she lived, dedicating herself devotedly to the service of God with fasts and prayers. She also rendered service with the same works as before, by grinding cereals, drawing water, and gathering wood in the countryside, while her feet were being injured by the pricking of thorns, by sharp splinters of wood, and by small stones, until they bled abundantly. Those who saw that blood on the way said to one another, "This blood is from Walatta-Petros."

She and her companions also used to go to the harvested fields in order to glean leftover grain; they would collect it for their sustenance. When she started to glean, after a little while her basket would suddenly fill up for her. Even though she would pour its contents into a leather sack or another basket, they would not harmfully diminish because God's blessing was in her hands. Those other sisters would glean only a small quantity, however.

One time, when the owner of the field came and saw her gleanings as opposed to theirs, he reviled her and said about her, "She has stolen from my sheaves, that was how she so quickly filled it!"

Then, injuriously, he scattered all that she had gathered on the ground. She was not sad, however, and did not grumble at all when he reviled her and harmed her by pouring it out, but was patient and accepted with praise for God all that happened to her.

Chapter 15: Our Mother Preaches and Incurs the King's Wrath

[122]

While our holy Mother Walatta-Petros lived like this in that region of Tsiyaat, she became animated by religious zeal and could not contain it. She exhorted the people of the town not to accept the filthy faith of Pope Leo and not to mention the name of the apostate king during the Liturgy since he was outside the true faith and accursed. As Paul says, "If an angel from above taught you something different from that which we have taught you, let him be accursed."

When King Susinyos heard about this talk, he became extremely angry and exceedingly furious. He roared like a lion and threatened Walatta-Petros's brothers and other relatives. He proclaimed against them, "I call the sky and the earth as witnesses against you! I swear by my mighty kingdom that I will punish you, that you will die a terrible death, and that I will purge your memory from the earth if you don't quickly bring in Walatta-Petros. Behold, with her words she has stripped me of my kingship, rebelled against me, betrayed me, and insulted me as well as my faith. She has subverted the hearts of that town's people so that they don't accept my faith and don't mention my name in the Liturgy. Before, there was no enmity between you and me. From now on, though, I have a feud with you!"

When Walatta-Petros's relatives heard the threats that the king spoke against them, they became very afraid and were shaken because that king was fierce. He did not show clemency to anyone; as he said he would do, he would do.

So they sent her these words, "Behold, all of us will perish on account of you! None of us will be spared, neither young nor old, because the king is angry indeed and has proclaimed against us and promised us death. He has said to us, 'Walatta-Petros has stripped me of my kingship and rebelled against me. If you don't bring her in quickly, you will die a terrible death.' Now we say to you: Come quickly, don't tarry, and don't determine our death, because you are flesh from our flesh and bone from our bone: your mother and your brothers."

When she heard this message, our holy Mother Walatta-Petros became very sad and took counsel with her companions. All of them together, unanimously, said, "We prefer to go and die for our [123] faith than that our relatives die on our account. Do we not hope and wait for this anyway? Our faith is with us in our hearts; no one can rob us of it. As the Gospel says about the sister of Lazarus, 'As for Mary, she has chosen the good part, which will not be taken away from her.'"

Having said these things, they set out from there and returned to her familial home. There our holy Mother Walatta-Petros met with her mother and her brothers. They implored her, "Do not violate the word of the king, so that he will not kill you and us because of your rebelling."

What is more, her mother lifted her breasts and said to her, "Am I not your mother who nurtured you with these breasts of mine? Do you have no regard for me?"

However, our holy Mother Walatta-Petros did not listen to their words and did not bend her mind to their advice. As the apostles say, "Is it right that we should listen to you and not to God? We prefer to please God than to please men."

Chapter 16: Our Mother Appears Before King Susinyos

At that time, the king was in his castle. He ordered that her relatives bring her to him, so they took her in. She went, hoping to die for the true faith. With her went her mother and her brothers; they followed her in tears, as if they were seeing her off to death, like a corpse that is taken away to be buried.

Our holy Mother Walatta-Petros did not lift her face and did not look at them, however, but rather said to them, "Why do you cry and break my heart? Why do you place an obstacle in my way? Do not cry for me but rather cry over yourselves. Truly, from now on nothing bothers me. Truly, I carry the suffering of Christ in my flesh.

"'Who can make me abandon my love for Christ? Suffering? Tribulation? Exile, hunger, nakedness, the sword, anguish?' As scripture says, 'Because of you, Lord, they will kill us every day. We have become like sheep that will be slaughtered.' 'I am confident, however, that nothing can make me abandon the love for God through Jesus Christ: neither death, nor life; neither angels, nor nobles; neither what is, nor what will come; neither someone powerful, nor anything above nor the abyss,' not even being born again in hell. There is nothing that can make me abandon the love of Christ. As for me, I will always be faithful and will never renege. Nobody whosoever can persuade my heart that I should renounce my faith, whether they frighten me with banishment to remote places, put me into the fire, throw me to the lions, drown me in Lake Tana, cut up my body and my limbs, or punish me with each and every sort of torture. Still, I will never renounce my faith. Rather, I am strong of heart through the word of our Lord Jesus Christ, who says, 'Do not fear those who kill your flesh. Your soul nobody can kill. Rather, fear him who has permission, after having killed, to put soul and body together into the fire of hell.'"

[124]

Continuing on her way, our holy Mother Walatta-Petros then arrived at the king's castle. The king ordered all the great lords, nobles, learned men, and judges to assemble, and they did as the king had commanded. They all assembled, richly adorned, in great magnificence, and sat down in a circle, according to their ranks and orders. Then the king commanded that they bring in our holy Mother Walatta-Petros. She came and stood in front of them with a determined heart and a strong faith. She did not tremble due to their magnificence, the great number of their assembly, or their empty talk. As David says in Psalms, "Why are the gentiles in uproar, and why do the people make empty talk? The kings of the earth have risen up, and the rulers have conspired with them against God and against his Anointed One."

[125]   Walatta-Petros, by contrast, stood alone, according to the procedure for a rebel against the king. Then those charged with speaking for the king—while he stayed in another room—said to her, "You have rebelled against the king, you have rebelled against God. You have resisted his order, you have transgressed against his word, and you have blasphemed against his faith. You have subverted the hearts of the people of the land so that they don't accept his faith and don't mention his name in the Liturgy!"

However, our holy Mother Walatta-Petros did not respond or reply at all. Rather, she listened with her head bowed and a critical smile, but humbly said, "I have not reviled the king. Rather, I will never renounce my faith."

On his part, the king regularly sent servants to inquire, "What does she say?"

They told him, "She does not respond at all. Rather, she keeps silent and expresses amusement."

Upon that, the king became enraged and said, "She despises me, laughs at me, and mocks me," and ordered that she be killed or at least her breasts cut off.

At that point Walatta-Petros's husband Malkiya-Kristos stood up before the king and said to him soothingly, "My lord, do not lose your temper. It is not due to contempt for you that she is laughing. Rather, an evil spirit that has been residing in her since her childhood makes her laugh."

With these words, Malkiya-Kristos calmed the king's rage. Truly, Malkiya-Kristos still loved Walatta-Petros very much. As for our holy Mother Walatta-Petros, she did not fear death and was not terrified by the king's majesty. As Peter says, "Do not fear that which strikes you with awe, and do not be terrified by it. Rather,

[127]   sanctify God with all your heart." So Walatta-Petros prayed, "You who have strengthened the prophets, strengthen me! You who have strengthened the apostles, strengthen me! You who have strengthened the martyrs, strengthen me so that I die for the sake of your name and receive the crown of martyrdom."

The king's counselors then advised him, "Hear us, O King! It is better for you to abandon the idea of killing a woman than to have her entire lineage, the house of Dawaro and Fatagar, as your enemies."

The king replied, "If she leaves me alone and keeps quiet, leave her alone."

All of this happened, however, because it did not please God for [128] her to walk down this path of martyrdom. Rather, he had prepared another path for her, namely, the path of Anthony and Macarius, the holy monks of old, just as the monk before her conception had said that she would guard his flocks. Truly, our Lord says, "My Father has many dwelling places."

They let her go then, but told her, "Don't go to a faraway region, and don't teach again. Rather, stay with your family." So her family took her and made her live with them.

Chapter 17: Our Mother Escapes Duke Silla-Kristos

Then many theological teachers who were of the true faith came there. They found comfort in Walatta-Petros's presence, and encouragement through each other.

Soon thereafter, she fled again and entered the monastic settlement of Zagé. With her were Walatta-Pawlos, Eheta-Kristos, and many others, as well as her maidservants Iyopraxia, Maryamaweet, and Eskindiraweet. Father Tsigé-Haymanot was also there with them. He used to comfort and encourage them. They lived together in peace.

Then a wily man came there deceitfully, under the guise of a friend wanting to visit them, just like in the story about the man who once visited Father Babnooda in Egypt. They did not understand that he had come in bad faith, however, and offered him good food, which he ate. Then he took a little of that food and [129] wrapped it up in his clothes to take home and show to others. Now he left immediately.

When he came home, he took that food out of his clothes to show to his wife. However, while he held it in his hand, an angel of God snatched the food away from him. He was shocked and bewildered, and therefore told his wife what he had done. She became irritated with him and said to him, "Why did you act like that and seek out divine punishment for yourself?"

Also, Duke Silla-Kristos sent one of his soldiers as a spy to investigate our holy Mother Walatta-Petros's situation at Zagé. The solider arrived and met with them. They gave him food to eat also, which he ate. Now, imagine, that soldier was a son of Eheta-Kristos's husband!

Then the soldier left and reported back to Silla-Kristos what he had seen and that he had eaten fine, delicious, and good-smelling food. He added, "My lord, you worry needlessly. Walatta-Petros's situation is better than even yours!"

When Silla-Kristos heard this, he gnashed his teeth and longed to mount a surprise attack against them. At that time, he was at Dabra Entonyos.

When our holy Mother Walatta-Petros heard about this, she hurriedly left Zagé and headed toward Abbabeet in a boat. In that part of the lake, there were three large hippopotamuses. One of them broke away from the group and, snorting, approached with the intention of overturning their boat and drowning them.

The boatmen as well as the sisters who were with Walatta-Petros were afraid and exclaimed, "Let us throw ourselves overboard, of our own volition, so that this hippo will not drown us!"

Our holy Mother Walatta-Petros, however, scolded them, "Do not be afraid, O you of little faith! What makes you fear? Do you think that you will never die? Whether you throw yourselves overboard or whether that hippopotamus overturns you, you will die one and the same death. Take heart and don't be afraid."

When fear completely gripped them, however, Walatta-Petros covered them with her nun's leather cloak while she prayed in her heart the *Salama Malaak*. Meanwhile, that hippopotamus came ever closer, eventually setting its front feet on the boat and yawning open its mouth. Our holy Mother Walatta-Petros, how-

[131]

ever, was not afraid at all but counted its teeth: their number was nine.

After the hippopotamus had hung on for a while, it pulled down its feet and turned back, fleeing as though someone was following and chasing it from behind, until it disappeared from view. It did not reunite with its companions; it remained unknown where it went.

Do you see, my loved ones, what wonders God worked for our holy Mother Walatta-Petros because of the strength of her faith? As scripture says, "God works wonders for his saints." And, "Blessed is the man who puts his trust in the name of God."

On that day, Walatta-Petros emerged from the lake safe and sound and reached the place she wanted, Abbabeet. There she remained for a few days and then returned to Zagé.

Chapter 18: Our Mother Moves from the Zagé Monastic Settlement to a Waldeba Monastery [132]

Then, when the European soldiers searching and lying in wait for her became many, our holy Mother Walatta-Petros fled from Zagé together with the sisters she was in charge of; she wanted to go to Waldeba. She left Father Tsigé-Haymanot behind, hiding her secret plan from him. She did not reveal it to him so that he would not stand in her way nor prevent her from going.

Later though, when he found out that she had left, he followed her and tracked her, asking around and inquiring about where she had gone. Eventually he found her on the road and took a stand against her to prevent her from going; he entreated and condemned her. She did not obey him, however. She did not accept his words but instead continued on her way. Nevertheless, he did not stop following her.

So our holy Mother Walatta-Petros said to him, with words of reprimand, "Why won't you return home? What business do you have with me, and what do you want from me? Have you not heard what the book with instructions for monks says, 'First of all, righteous men and monks should stay away from women'?"

When she said this to him, he was pained in his heart, but also angry. So he left her and returned home.

As for our holy Mother Walatta-Petros, she kept on walking, ever so slowly, on her delicate feet, ascending steep passes and descending steep slopes, sometimes crawling like children do, with blood flowing from her delicate feet. They were all numb from walking on rough and rugged roads. When she was no longer able to walk, she wrapped her feet in pieces of cloth.

Progressing in this manner, around noon, she arrived at a place where there was no water. She rested in the shade of a tree and wanted to stay there. Meanwhile, the disciples who were with her were looking for water but did not find any. So they became agitated and desperate and said to our holy Mother Walatta-Petros, "Let us leave this place so that we do not perish from thirst!"

[134] She, however, replied, "O you of little faith! Why are you agitated and desperate?" Then she turned her head and pointed with her fingers, "I say to you, 'Go and search over there, and water will not be found wanting.'"

Having gone to that nearby place she had pointed out to them, her disciples found a spring of clear water that was surrounded by high cacti on all sides. They drank from that water and were happy. Through the prayers of our holy Mother Walatta-Petros, the water had gushed out at a place where none had been before.

Then Walatta-Petros entered Waldeba. There she lived, dedicating herself devotedly to the service of God with fasts and prayers, while strenuously exerting herself spiritually and through many virtuous deeds, through toil and labor. As scripture says, "He who has toiled in this world will live forever. Truly, he will not see decay."

Chapter 19: Our Mother Assists the Wicked Old Woman

Meanwhile, an extremely ill-tempered old woman also lived there; she would constantly be angry. No one could bear her wicked character. She did not express thanks when the sisters attended to her and never blessed them when they worked for her. They could never satisfy her. Rather, she insulted and reviled them. So all the sisters of the monastic settlement kept away from her, and she lived alone in great misery. None of the sisters would go to see her.

When our holy Mother Walatta-Petros then saw the old woman's entire disposition and all the misery she suffered, she girded herself with the belt of faith, wrapped herself in the cloth of humility, and began to serve her like a maidservant, with a determined heart. She became the old woman's helper and placed herself under her feet: she ground flour, baked bread, and drew water. When she lacked grain, she went gleaning, returning with it to sustain the old woman. She fulfilled the old woman's every wish.

The old woman showed no gratitude for Walatta-Petros's work, however, but rather was always angry, reviling and insulting her, "You, girl, are a thief! Although you outwardly pose as a righteous woman, inside you are a wicked serpent."

When Walatta-Petros baked bread, she would use her hands, burning them on the red-hot, flaming oven until they peeled. Then the old woman would reprimand her, "How did your mother raise [135] you? How did she teach you and train you in this terrible way of doing things?"

Every day, the old woman would speak many insulting and derisive words like this against Walatta-Petros. Our holy mother would not be distressed, however, and would not grumble because of all this, but would bear it happily and patiently, emulating the long-suffering monk John the Short.

One day when Eheta-Kristos overheard the old woman heaping insults on Walatta-Petros, she wept copiously and said to Walatta-Petros, "What is your business with this old woman so that you serve her even though she abuses and insults you? Is there no other work than this that pleases God?"

Our holy Mother Walatta-Petros replied, "Don't weep on my behalf. All that abuse does not come from her but from Satan. As for me, it does not distress me. Rather, I consider it a benefit and a blessing. Truly, the Gospel says, 'Woe are you when people say nice things about you' and praise you."

Then, when Walatta-Petros had completed a year serving her, the old woman passed away. Our holy Mother Walatta-Petros shrouded her corpse with her own hands and buried her.

See then, my loved ones, the extraordinary gifts Walatta-Petros had been given! O what humility! O what goodness! O what patience! Being a noblewoman, of her own free will she made herself into a servant of one who was inferior to her and reviled her, so as to attain through her the crown of the long-suffering martyrs. Truly, he who loves the stinging bee will taste the honey. Conversely, he who does not love her and flees from her will not taste the honey.

Likewise, our holy Mother Walatta-Petros loved this old woman and subjected herself to her, because by virtue of her she could taste the sweetness of the Kingdom of Heaven. Moreover, if she had not subjugated herself to this old woman, later, the kings and great lords would not have submitted to her, and the demons would not have conceded defeat before her.

[136] As John Saba, the Syrian Spiritual Elder says, "If Joseph had not first subjected himself to slavery, he would not have become lord over the land of Egypt." Also, Paul says, "Working in the flesh brings benefit for a short time, but righteousness gives power in everything, and in it lies hope for life in this world and in the one to come." Woe and doubly woe are we who do not act likewise and do not subjugate ourselves. Let alone those who abuse and curse us, not even those who praise and bless us do we serve properly. Even though we are in good health, we say that we are sick to avoid serving, and even though we have strength, we say that we are weak, and we make many excuses.

Chapter 20: Our Mother Receives Food and a Message from Her Mother

Listen up: We again want to tell you the story of our holy Mother Walatta-Petros, how for six months she lived in that monastic settlement in Waldeba, sustaining herself on green leaves only, together with Eheta-Kristos and with all the women who were with her, until their teeth changed from being white to resembling those greens.

One day, when our holy Mother Walatta-Petros saw Eheta-Kristos's teeth, she asked her, "My sister, what has happened to your teeth?"

Eheta-Kristos retorted, "The same as to yours!"

As scripture says, "They lived in misery and hardship and suffering. They experienced what one should never experience and roamed the mountains, the wildernesses, caves, and pits of the earth." [137]

Then Walatta-Petros's mother Kristos-Ebayaa dispatched to them many donkeys loaded with flour and every sort of necessary provision. The dispatched servants arrived at Waldeba, and all the sisters were happy when they saw this because they had gone hungry for a period of six months; it appeared to them that now they would eat. They told our holy Mother Walatta-Petros about the food.

Upon hearing this, however, she became very sad and said, "What have I done to anger God so that he has brought upon me that which I have run away from?"

The sisters said to her, "We are happy and eager to eat. Why are you distressed?"

She replied, "Me? I am distressed because it looks to me like something that Satan has brought upon us to tempt us because he is deceitful. He tempted our Lord likewise, as the Gospel reports, 'He fasted forty days and forty nights. Then he was hungry, and the Tempter approached him.' He wants to put us to the test as well with this temptation."

The sisters then said to her, "Shall the dispatched servants come and tell you the message they bring?"

Our holy Mother Walatta-Petros replied, "No, today they shall spend the night outside our compound. For dinner, they can eat from the flour they have brought. Today I will not listen to their message nor receive anyone of them."

So the servants spent the night outside; they kept on waiting for three days. As for Walatta-Petros, she locked her hut and kept praying to God that he reveal to her the reason for their coming. God answered her prayers, and she understood that their coming was God's will because he is compassionate toward the afflicted and the hungry. As we have already mentioned before, when Samson was hungry he prayed to God, obtained honey from the mouth of a lion, and ate it. God furthermore fed Elijah through the beak of a raven, and, when they had thrown Daniel into a pit, God sent Habakkuk with bread to Daniel because hunger tormented him.

[138]   Therefore, on the third day, our holy Mother Walatta-Petros said to Eheta-Kristos, "Summon the dispatched servants and accept the provisions they have brought." Eheta-Kristos went and summoned them.

They entered the compound and told Walatta-Petros the following message from her mother, "Come immediately, because I long to see you! Also, I have something that I want to talk with you about face-to-face. What makes you so stubborn? Am I not your mother who carried you in my womb and who nurtured you with my breasts? Do I happen to have another daughter than you, either older or younger than you? May the peace of God be with us, amen!"

After having listened, our holy Mother Walatta-Petros remained silent and did not respond to them. The sisters then urged her, "Give them a return message so they can go home."

So she replied to the dispatched servants, "Say the following to my mother, 'It would not be right for me to abandon the monastic settlement and return to the world, which I left. Rather, it would be right for you to follow your daughter to where she has gone.'" With these words she dispatched the messengers, and they returned home.

Eheta-Kristos then asked her, "How come you at first refused the sent food, and why did you later accept it?"

Our holy Mother Walatta-Petros replied, "I first refused it because it seemed to me that it came from Satan. Later, however, I accepted it since I understood that it had come by the will of God."

So then, understand and comprehend, my loved ones! For whom

would it be possible to show such endurance while being hungry, after not having tasted any proper food for six months? Which hungry person would not be eager to eat when seeing food? Leave aside someone whose mother sent provisions to him: I believe any hungry person would have gone even to strangers in order to beg or steal. Our holy Mother Walatta-Petros, however, was capable of rejecting food through the power of God. As Paul says, "I can master everything, destitution as well as luxury. I am accustomed to everything: to hunger as well as to abundance, to suffering as well as to joy. I can master everything because God has enabled me to do this."   [139]

Chapter 21: A Righteous Monk Predicts Our Mother Will Found Communities

In that monastic settlement of Waldeba, there lived a righteous monk whose name was Malkiya-Kristos. When he realized that the time of his passing away was near, he came to our holy Mother Walatta-Petros to tell her the day of his death and to take his leave of her. Truly, he knew what was hidden and what would happen before it happened.

As soon as he had informed her about the day of his death, our holy Mother Walatta-Petros became very distressed and said in her heart, "I wish God would let me die before this righteous man. How can he die and not me?" This thought was not right before God, however. Therefore, she immediately began to suffer a piercing pain and almost died, just like the biblical king Hezekiah had suffered and said, "Like a pelican I croak and like a dove I speak."

The monk was aware of what went through Walatta-Petros's mind and reprimanded her, "Why do you desire death and oppose God's judgment? Truly, it is he who multiplies or diminishes a person's time on earth. It is he who dispenses death and life according to his will; it does not happen due to human will. This is why such strong suffering has befallen you: in order to test you.

However, you will not die. From now on, do not think such a thought again.

"Listen up, I will tell you the word that God has put into my mouth: 'Through your stewardship, communities will be formed [140] seven times in seven places, and many souls will be saved through you. The first community will be that of Zhebey, the second that of Chanqwa, the third that of Mitsillé, the fourth that of Zagé (whose members will be killed by an epidemic), the fifth that of Damboza, the sixth that of Afer Faras, and the seventh that of Zambowl. Only after that will be your death.' And I further tell you: Constantly read the Gospel of John, since I have had a true vision that he who constantly reads it will be greatly honored. For him, a canopy of light will be erected above him, and an ornamented golden throne covered with carpets will be placed below him for his sake. That's why I tell you: Read this gospel all the days of your life!"

After the monk had told Walatta-Petros these and other similar things from among the secrets of God, he took his leave of her. He returned to his cell, parted from this world, and went to God who loved him. May his prayers and blessing be with us forever, amen.

Chapter 22: Our Mother Commands the Animals

It was customary for the monks of Waldeba to hold supplications: [141] they would beseech the Lord in prayer from July 6 to 12. Thereafter they would receive blessings from the elders among them, take leave of one another, and again go about their occupations in order to gain their daily bread. For that period, our holy Mother Walatta-Petros withdrew and separated herself from the sisters who were with her. She stayed near the monks' place in order to listen to the recitation of their supplications—without constructing a shelter for herself against either the rain or the sun until those months were completed, keeping vigil all night and day, all alone.

There was one disciple named Takla-Maryam who looked after her, ministered to her, and brought her bitter roots as her food.

Now he is the one about whom it has been said that he once found a large serpent in the shelter where he slept. When he saw it, he was terrified and afraid, and trembling went to our holy Mother Walatta-Petros.

When she saw him, she knew what was on his mind before he had spoken. She said to him, "What scares you? Go and lie down on top of the serpent. If it is God's will, it will be given power over you and you will not escape it. However, if it is not God's will, nothing will hurt you."

Obediently, he turned back, strew grass on the serpent, and lay down there. At the time, the serpent was underneath him, but did not attack him.

While our holy Mother Walatta-Petros lived in wilderness se-   [143] clusion, two wild animals of different species, a stag and an antelope, used to guard her at night, one at her head and the other at her feet. Each morning that disciple Takla-Maryam would come and find their tracks in the places where each of them had slept.

Chapter 23: Our Mother Debates with Jesus Christ and Receives His Promise

On one day during that period, while our holy Mother Walatta-Petros was praying with her arms stretched out, our Lord Jesus Christ—he be praised—came to her and greeted her, "Peace be with you."

He then took her hands in his and said to her, "You have no role in this monastic settlement of Waldeba, which is why you stay by yourself. Instead, you will leave it, and then many people will gather around you, from east and west. They will be pure doves, and they will benefit from you for the salvation of their souls. Not a single soul among them will be lost."

Our holy Mother Walatta-Petros replied, "How will this be possible for me to do? How will I be able to save others, I who cannot save myself? Am I not mud, and a pit of filthy sludge?"

Our Lord responded, "Even mud, when it is mixed with straw,

becomes strong and enduring and can hold grain. You, too, I will make likewise strong."

Walatta-Petros did not accept our Lord's words, however, and did not believe what he said. So he now made pure white doves come to her and descend all over her. They surrounded her completely, from her head to her feet. Some even entered into her tunic while others wanted to alight on her head, but she turned them away with her hands and collected them into her lap. He then said to her, "They are the ones whom I entrust to you so that you will take care of them."

Our holy Mother Walatta-Petros replied, "But I cannot take care of them! They will fly away and escape me." When she opposed him like this, he left her and ascended into heaven.

However, our Lord came again the next day and spoke to Walatta-Petros in the same way, and she too replied to him as before. Then, in a golden basket, he brought shining glass and crystal vessels [146] and said to her, "These are chosen vessels, which I hereby entrust to you to take care of on my behalf until I request them back from you and take them back to me."

She replied, "I cannot take care of them: they will break, and I will be held responsible!"

Our Lord responded, "Not even one of them will perish, because I will be in your midst." In this way, he spoke to her once, twice, thrice. Our holy Mother Walatta-Petros did not accept his words, however, and did not believe what he said. She was anxious that what had happened to Eve not happen to her.

Our Lord then gave Walatta-Petros a protective promise: "Heaven and earth will pass away but my word will not pass away. Not only those on the inside (who are in your care already), but also those on the outside (who will come from east and west to invoke your name): they will all be saved and will not perish! If you don't believe what I tell you, behold, I will send a lion and he will kill one of your disciples."

Having said this, our Lord left her, but things happened as he had proclaimed: A lion came, terrified and dispersed her disciples, and killed one of them. The others came running and rushing and amassed around her, falling over her and squeezing her so that she almost died.

She scolded them, saying, "What scares you? Do you really believe you will never die?" Then she rose and prayed together with them. Immediately the lion grew quiet and returned to his lair. Then the sisters also turned back and went to their huts, and our holy Mother Walatta-Petros remained behind alone.

Chapter 24: Our Mother Agrees to Found Seven Communities

[148]

Then our Lord came to her again and said to her, "Didn't I tell you, 'Leave this monastic settlement so that you can gather souls'? Saving only yourself won't help you. I have given you a protective promise: I will be with you and will help you to take care of all your followers. As I myself say in the Gospel, 'Where two or three are gathered in my name, there I am among them.' And if one day you so ask me, and you want someone who entered your community to die, I will do that for you and I will fulfill your wish."

He then again, as he had before, brought her those white doves and those glass and crystal vessels, saying to her, "Take care of them for me, for they are chosen vessels without any blemish. They are the souls of your sons and your daughters: whosoever enters into your house will not perish, and neither will your house disappear until the end of the world. This is the sign of the protective promise that is between me and you."

Finally, she then said to him, "Your will be done, O my Lord."

This is the behavior of the wise: they do not immediately believe someone when they are told what is going to happen. As Luke the Evangelist reports, "The angel said to him, 'Don't be afraid, Zacharias! Behold, your prayers have been heard and your wife Elizabeth will conceive and bear you a son, whom you will name John. He will be a joy unto you, and many will rejoice about his birth. For he will be great before God.' Zacharias said to the angel, 'How do I know that all this will happen? After all, I am old, and

[149]

also my wife's fertile days have passed.' The angel replied to him, 'I am Gabriel who stands before God! I have been sent to speak to you and announce this good news to you. Behold, now you will become mute and will be unable to speak because you have not believed my words, which will come true at the set time.' " And so it happened.

Luke further reports, regarding our Lady Mary, when the angel made the announcement to her, "he said to her, 'Don't be afraid, O Mary, for you have found favor with God. Behold, you will conceive and give birth to a son whom you will name Jesus. He will be great, and will be called the Son of God Most High.' " Then "Mary said to the angel, 'How can this happen to me since I have not known a man?' The angel responded, 'God's Holy Spirit will come over you, and the power of the Most High will overshadow you.' " He who will be born from you will be holy, " 'and will be called the Son of God Most High. Behold, even your relative Elizabeth has conceived and become pregnant with a child, despite her mature years; and behold, this is the sixth month for her, who had been called barren. For there is nothing that is impossible for God.' Now Mary said to the angel, 'Here I am, a maidservant of God. May it happen to me as you have told me.' " And so it happened.

Also, our holy Mother Walatta-Petros first resisted Christ because she thought he might be Satan. As Paul says, "For Satan disguises himself as an angel of light." Afterward, however, she accepted Christ when she saw a reliable sign from him. By contrast, when Eve immediately believed the word of the serpent—who promised her that she would become God by eating from the tree that enables one to discern good and evil—she became opposed to God. She therefore had to leave paradise and live in the land of thorns and thistles. She brought down death upon herself because God had told them before, "Do not eat from the tree that stands in the middle of paradise! For on the day on which you eat from it, you will become subject to death." Eve did not even get that which she had wanted, to become God. All this has been written for our protection and benefit.

[150]

Christ further told Walatta-Petros that she would go to the region of Zhebey where she would be imprisoned and guarded by a Black man, remaining there for three years; that she would become sick from the lowland fever; and that after this she would leave Zhebey.

See then, my loved ones, how God lets the saints know beforehand that they will encounter imprisonment, exile, and every type of tribulation from infidel kings on account of the true faith. As the Gospel says, "Behold, I send you as sheep among wolves." Furthermore, the Gospel says, after this, "They will seize you and take you to the tribunals, before the kings and great lords. This will happen to you for the sake of my name." Paul, too, says in the Acts of the Apostles, "Yet in various cities the Holy Spirit let me know, 'Suffering and shackles await you.'" And the Apostle Peter says in his letter, "However, for now, for a little while, you will have to suffer grief due to various tribulations, which will meet you as a test of your faith." Tribulations do not happen unexpectedly to the saints. Rather, they are told about them beforehand so that they can be steadfast with hope and understanding, protect themselves with the shield of faith, don the armor of righteousness, and shod themselves with the shoes of the Gospel. [151]

In just this way, in advance, God also informed our holy Mother Walatta-Petros about what would happen before it happened. By contrast, tribulations befall sinners unexpectedly. As Paul says, "You know very well that the Day of our Lord will arrive like the coming of a thief, at a time when those who deny him think that they are in safety and peace. Then, suddenly, destruction will come upon them, like labor pains upon a pregnant woman, and they will be unable to escape."

Chapter 25: Our Mother Discusses Christ's Promise

After the supplications ritual of Waldeba was finished, our holy Mother Walatta-Petros returned from seclusion and again joined her companions. Eheta-Kristos and Ghirmana asked her, "What did you experience, and what kind of visions have you seen since you withdrew from us over those months?"

She kept it hidden from them, however, and said, "As for me, I did not experience or see anything because the veil of sin covered me and the curtain of transgression screened me from any vision."

The two women kept asking her individually, however. Walatta-Petros became exasperated with them and did not tell them anything because she was afraid of empty praise. But they did not stop asking her; they implored and pressured her. So she lifted her mind up to God and spent many hours in silence. Then she obtained permission from God, and now she told them how our Lord had come to her and taken her hand; how he had told her everything that would happen, from the beginning to the end; how she had said to him, "I am mud. How can I do this?"; and how he had given her the protective promise.

Eheta-Kristos and Ghirmana were witnesses and have told us what Walatta-Petros said. Likewise, the disciple Takla-Maryam was her witness as well, and the testimony of all three agrees. We [152] know that their testimony is true. We certainly have not written lies, nor have we used ingenious fables to acquaint you with the story of our holy Mother Walatta-Petros's glory. Rather, we know and are certain that the testimony of two or three people is trustworthy. We ourselves, too, have seen as we have heard.

Chapter 26: Our Mother Preaches and Works Miracles

Thus, our holy Mother Walatta-Petros lived, teaching the people of Waldeba the true faith and exhorting them not to accept the filthy faith of the Europeans. When King Susinyos heard this news about her, he secretly sent out spies to keep an eye on her. However, people told our holy Mother Walatta-Petros that spies sent by the king were approaching. Therefore, she, together with her companions, withdrew from that place where she had lived until then and set up camp in a dry riverbed, since it was the dry season.

She had the *Faith of the Fathers* with her, as well as other books. One day it then rained very hard, so much so that the riverbed was filled with water instantly. It streamed down and overflowed the people and the books. Yet it did not damage the books at all; not even a single letter of them was wiped out. They remained intact thanks to the powerful help of our holy Mother Walatta-Petros; they remained unaffected. Thereafter, she returned to her previous abode in Waldeba.

Listen up, again we will tell you about our holy Mother Walatta-Petros's perfect virtue and how God worked miracles and wonders for her. When a tapeworm had appeared in her belly, the sisters prepared a medicine for her to drink so that she would expel the tapeworm. While they were carefully treating her, a man came by who also was plagued by tapeworm, and had been for quite a while because he lacked the medicine to drink. He asked that they give him that medicine and told them how tapeworm had plagued him. When she heard this, our holy Mother Walatta-Petros felt compassion for him, abstained from drinking the medicine, gave it to him, and he drank it. However, she also recovered, even before him, without drinking, and the tapeworm never again appeared in her. [153]

Have you ever seen such a love of one's neighbor and such a surrendering of one's own means of deliverance to another soul? As Christ says, "Blessed is he who surrenders himself in redemption of his neighbor." This is a great gift of charity, greater than all others.

Thereafter, God sent a scourge to Waldeba, a wild beast called a *shilhoolhoot*. It would come at night to where people slept, pierce their heads, and eat their brains.

Because of this frightful development, terror and tumult gripped all the sisters, and they said to our holy Mother Walatta-Petros, "It's impossible for us to remain here due to that dumb beast's great, awe-inspiring power! Even a locked door does not prevent it from entering because it comes through the roof of the house. Not even lions or snakes scare us like this beast does! Let us leave and go to another place. If you refuse, we will scatter on our own and leave you behind alone!" [154]

When they spoke to her like this, together with them she left that place and went to the region of Tsellemt. There, too, she lived teaching the inhabitants the true faith and exhorting them not to adopt the filthy faith of the Europeans.

Chapter 27: Our Mother Again Incurs the King's Wrath

Then, when King Susinyos heard that our holy Mother Walatta-Petros was in the district of Tsellemt and that she was teaching the Orthodox faith, he became angry and enraged, roaring like a lion.

He said, "Even though I left her alone, she doesn't leave me alone! Even though I was lenient toward her, she's not lenient toward me. From now on, however, I will decide on my own what to do with her."

So he summoned one of his military men, whose name was Commander Filaatawos and who was in charge of that district of Tsellemt. He said to him, "Go and bring Walatta-Petros to me quickly!"

Filaatawos went as the king had commanded him, arrived at where she stayed, and said to her, "The king has ordered me to you. He says to you, 'Come immediately, and don't say, "Tomorrow!"'"

Our holy Mother Walatta-Petros replied, "Behold, I am in your hands. Do with me as the king has ordered. I am ready for it and prepared to die. I'm not afraid of anything."

Immediately then, our holy Mother Walatta-Petros set off from there and went with him. With her were the sisters Eheta-Kristos and Kristos-Sinnaa, as well as her maidservants Maryamaweet and Eskindiraweet.

[155]   ### Chapter 28: The Europeans Try to Convert Our Mother

Walatta-Petros arrived at and entered the king's castle in the month of May. They lodged her in the house of General Billa-Kristos. Then they began to try to persuade her with many clever tricks to abandon the true faith of the Orthodox pope Dioscoros and adopt the filthy faith of the Catholic pope.

Three renowned European false teachers came to her and debated with her about their filthy faith, which says, "Christ still has two natures after the ineffable union of his humanity and divinity."

She argued with them, defeated them, and embarrassed them. Each morning, other Europeans came to her, reading to her and explaining their filthy doctrinal book to her. Our holy Mother Walatta-Petros, however, did not listen to their talk and did not accept their faith. Rather, she laughed and made fun of them.

As the Gospel says, "Therefore, you all should not call yourselves teachers on this earth because your teacher is one, Christ." Also, the Apostle John in his letter says, "Our brothers, do not believe every spirit, but test the spirit, whether it is from God, because many false prophets have come into the world" who do not believe in Jesus Christ, that he has come in the flesh. "By this [156] you will know the Spirit of God: each spirit that believes in Jesus Christ, that he came in the flesh of a man, is from God, but each spirit that does not believe in Jesus Christ, that he came in the flesh, is not from God. Rather, it is from the false messiah of whom you have heard that he would come." John further says, "Anyone who wavers and does not remain in the teaching of Christ is not with God. But he who remains in the teaching of Christ is in the Father and the Son. He who comes to you and does not bring this teaching, do not let him enter your houses and do not even greet him because he who greets him has fellowship with him in his evil deeds." This is why our holy Mother Walatta-Petros treated these European false teachers with contempt and repudiated them.

The king then inquired about her, "What does she say?"

The Europeans replied to him, "She does not listen and does not accept what we say. Instead, she insults us. Can water penetrate a heart of stone?"

Because of this, the king became enraged and wanted to kill her.

His counselors prevented him, however, saying, "Do not do something like that! If you kill her here, everyone will follow her and join her in death. And once the people have perished, over whom will you rule? Instead, order that she remain a captive."

So the king ordered that she be taken to the lowland region of Zhebey and handed over to the Black man living there, the king's subaltern, so that she would live there as a captive.

Following this decision, Malkiya-Kristos entered into the king's chamber, stood before him, and implored him, "My lord king, I beseech you, if I find grace before you, hand Walatta-Petros over to me until the months of the rainy season are over. During that time, I will admonish and advise her. In addition, the spiritual [157] leader of the Europeans, Afonsu, shall read his doctrinal book to her and have her listen to it every day. If then she still refuses to convert, we will send her away."

The king replied, "Yes, I agree to your proposal."

Our holy Mother Walatta-Petros was then handed over to Malkiya-Kristos. He took her to Azezo, lodged her in his house, and provided her with food. With her were Eheta-Kristos and Walatta-Kristos. Throughout their entire lives, Walatta-Petros and Eheta-Kristos were like our Lady Mary and Salome.

Afonsu went to Walatta-Petros each Saturday morning, without breaking for lunch, in a clever move to make her fast likewise, [158] and read his doctrinal book to her. However, he would return embarrassed because she treated him with contempt, repudiated him, and did not listen to his teaching.

Each time, the king asked, "Has Walatta-Petros converted and embraced our faith?"

But they responded, "No."

Chapter 29: King Susinyos Banishes Our Mother to Zhebey

Then, when the months of the rainy season had passed and November had begun, and the time was near that our Lord had predicted to her, "You will go down to Zhebey," the king summoned one of his military men and said to him, "Go and take Walatta-

Petros, her alone, to the region of Zhebey. Do not let anyone follow her, neither men nor women."

Having received the king's order, the soldier went, arrived at where our holy Mother Walatta-Petros was at Azezo and told her, "The king has ordered me to take you to the region of Zhebey."

Our holy Mother Walatta-Petros replied to him, "Here I am, in your hands. Do as the king has ordered."

At this time, Walatta-Kristos became afraid and fled, carrying a water container and wearing the clothes of a maidservant, like one who is going to draw water. Eheta-Kristos, on the other hand, remained behind at that place, Azezo. So our holy Mother Walatta-Petros went away alone, just as our Lord Jesus Christ had gone to Calvary alone, carrying his cross; she was like him. As Paul says, "Let us follow Christ's example in order to proceed from glory to glory."

Now, that soldier was very rough and of bad character, without mercy and fear of God. He took Walatta-Petros, made her mount a recalcitrant mule, and did not hold the reins for her but rather drove the mule from behind, poking at its anus with a stick so that it would become angry and throw her down, and she would die. He did not feel any compassion for her at all because Satan had rendered him hard-hearted. Acting thus, he took her down a rough and rugged road and beat that mule so hard that it fell and tumbled down a precipice. Immediately, though, an angel caught our holy Mother Walatta-Petros, laying her down on good land in soft grass so that she stood up alive and unharmed. [160]

As Saint Yared's book of hymns says, "Having taken three names, I lean on a staff. Even if I fall, I stand up again." Likewise, David says in Psalms, "Many are the sufferings of the righteous. However, God delivers them from everything. God protects all their bones, not one of them will be shattered inside them." He furthermore says, "Truly, for your sake God has ordered his angels to guard you in all your ways. They will lift you up with their hands so that your feet will not trip over a stone." In addition, Paul says, "We have a treasure in an earthen vessel, which shows that the great power is from God, not from us. While we suffer from everything, we are not distressed; while we are despised, we do not feel disgraced; while we are persecuted, we do not feel cast out; while we are tormented, we do not perish. We always carry the death of Christ in our flesh, so that the life of Christ may be known through this mortal body of ours." The same also happened to our holy Mother Walatta-Petros.

Chapter 30: Our Mother in Exile Earns the Fear of Her Guard

After this, the soldier made Walatta-Petros mount the mule again and brought her to the lowland region of Zhebey. He handed her over to the Black man, whom he told all the king's orders. The soldier said to him, "Guard her until the time when the king orders either her death or her life."

So she was alone. When her mother Kristos-Ebayaa heard that Walatta-Petros had gone away alone, she became very distressed. Then she sent her maidservant Ilarya to her so that she would stay with Walatta-Petros and serve her.

[161] The Black man then took charge of Walatta-Petros, did as the king had ordered him, and cast our holy Mother Walatta-Petros into prison. She spent three days without eating or drinking because the Black man was an impure heathen who had nothing in common with her, be it in way of life or in faith. She did not understand his words when he spoke with her, whether they were kind or cruel.

How terrible was this day and how difficult this hour in which our holy Mother Walatta-Petros suffered tribulation and banishment! It was much worse and much more difficult than any tribulation and banishment that met the other Orthodox Christians in those years. Where is she among women who is equal to Walatta-Petros? Who could have patiently born all this like her? Not only a weak woman, but even men who possess strength—they would not have been able to endure like Walatta-Petros. However, the power of God that was upon her enabled her to endure and gave her strength. As the Apostle Peter says, "After you have suffered for a little while, God will perfect you, strengthen you, and make you understand." If, by contrast, Walatta-Petros had been made to stay in a region of Christians whose language she would have understood, whose way of life she would have known, and with whom she could have participated in eating and drinking, her endurance would not have been extraordinary and difficult, but easy.

When the Black man saw her abstaining, he said to her in his language, "What's the matter with you? What is this you're doing, that you don't eat and drink? How will you stay alive?"

Unfortunately, there was no one who could translate between them. Suddenly, however, God opened Walatta-Petros's ears and she understood his language. As scripture says, "The Lord granted Joseph a sign as he went to the land of Egypt, and he understood a language that he had not known before." The same happened to her.

Therefore, our holy Mother Walatta-Petros replied to the Black man, "How can I, a Christian woman, eat food that you have prepared? How can I drink water from a cup that you drink from, you, an impure heathen who does not share my faith? You don't have any sacred prohibitions: you eat mice and serpents and all the impure animals that the Law has forbidden people to touch and eat. So bring me raw food, an unused pot for cooking, and an unused gourd for drawing water!" [162]

He, too, understood her language now. So he did accordingly and brought Walatta-Petros what she had requested. Ilarya then cooked that food and served it to her, but Walatta-Petros tasted only a little of it and then left the rest. Ilarya cried bitterly because our holy Mother Walatta-Petros had refrained from eating. The two of them lived for a month in this way, all by themselves.

Then Satan entered into the heart of the Black man so that he laid his eyes on Walatta-Petros: he began to make advances toward her, as men do with women. When she rejected him, he used a cord to tie her back to the house post and secured her in that position. He then gathered wood and brought fire to light the wood near her feet and torment her with the smoke. That fire went out, however: it did not burn and did not smoke. Therefore, when he failed, he let her go, untying the ropes from around her.

He did not stop making advances toward Walatta-Petros, however, and one day he went to see her at the prompting of Satan, thinking that he would be able to fulfill his desire to have her. But when he entered the hut where our holy and chosen Mother Walatta-Petros lived, he saw her standing in prayer, with her face resplendent like the sun. With her, by her side, stood an angel of God, holding a drawn sword in his hand near her ear.

Instantly, the Black man was shocked and scared. He retreated, falling on his back. From that day onward, he was chastened and did not make advances toward Walatta-Petros again. Rather, he treated her with respect and was afraid of her. Satan, too, was humiliated and defeated. How could that Black man aspire to what he aspired to? An act that was not even granted to Walatta-Petros's husband Malkiya-Kristos—did he imagine that it would be granted to him, a foul servant? However, that idea was not his own but Satan's, because in his insolence he wanted to become Lord.

[164]

Chapter 31: The Queen Helps Eheta-Kristos to Rejoin Our Mother

As for Eheta-Kristos, as soon as she was separated from Walatta-Petros, she cried and wailed day and night because she had remained behind alone and because her mother, holy and blessed Walatta-Petros, had left her. She was like an infant whom they had made leave its mother's breast. So she went to her majesty Queen Amata-Kristos and stood before her, crying and weeping bitterly.

Therefore, Amata-Kristos asked her, "What makes you weep, my woman?"

Eheta-Kristos replied, "I weep because I have been separated from my Mother Walatta-Petros and made to remain behind alone. So, I beg you now, my lady, if I find grace before you, have mercy on me. Look upon my sorrow, and on my behalf request Malkiya-

Kristos to dispatch me so that I can go to my mother Walatta-Petros."

Amata-Kristos felt compassion for Eheta-Kristos. She summoned Malkiya-Kristos and, as Eheta-Kristos had requested, asked him and got him to agree.

Malkiya-Kristos then went to the king, stood before him, and said to him, "Long may you live, my lord king! I have seen something amazing and witnessed something extraordinary that happened in your kingdom today."

The king inquired, "What have you seen and witnessed?"

Malkiya-Kristos replied, "Most people, when oppressed, exiled, and separated from their family, cry and grieve. That woman, though, who used to live with Walatta-Petros, cries and wails when we tell her, 'Live with your family in your own land.'" [165]

The king said to him, "So then, what do *you* suggest we do with her?"

Malkiya-Kristos responded, "I suggest that we send her to that region Zhebey so that the lowland fever may kill her, and so that she will not perpetually cause us trouble and annoy us."

The king was pleased with this proposal and said to Malkiya-Kristos, "Let it be as you have said."

So Malkiya-Kristos emerged from the king's hall and told Eheta-Kristos, "Hereby, we give you permission: Go!"

When Eheta-Kristos heard this, she sank down, kissed Malkiya-Kristos's feet, rejoiced and was so happy, thanking God. Then she arose, went forth, and reached the region where our holy and chosen Mother Walatta-Petros was. Eheta-Kristos found her and kissed her in greeting. But when she noticed how Walatta-Petros's appearance had darkened and her body had become emaciated, Eheta-Kristos hugged her and cried over her.

Our holy Mother Walatta-Petros consoled her, however, "What makes you cry, now that you have found me? Was it not me that you were looking for? From now on, rather, we should rejoice and thank God, who has arranged for us to live together in one place and has not let you and me be separated." By saying this, she made Eheta-Kristos stop crying.

Thereafter, Eheta-Kristos and Ilarya spent their days serving Walatta-Petros and preparing what she would eat and drink. Our holy Mother Walatta-Petros for her part spent her time applying herself devotedly to the service of God.

Chapter 32: Our Mother and the Miracle of the Serpent

Thereafter, Walatta-Petros's two disciples Takla-Maryam and Atsqa-Hawaryaat arrived. From then on, they would go regularly to Walatta-Petros's mother, brothers, and other relatives to collect various belongings and fine garments and bring them to her. One day Takla-Maryam went to Walatta-Petros's mother, collected many things, loaded them onto a donkey, and turned back toward Zhebey.

[166]

While he was walking on a path in the wilderness, evening overtook him and he found no house in which he could stay as a guest. So he took shelter under a tree that had grown above the lair of a serpent. He took the load from the donkey and then tied him to the tree, which stood on top of the serpent's lair. Takla-Maryam then lay down there without noticing the serpent and fell asleep. At the break of dawn, that serpent then hissed, crawled about, and shook the tree.

When the disciple saw the serpent, he was shocked and afraid. He quickly untied the donkey, loaded him with the valuables, and left, running. He believed that the serpent would pursue him. If that serpent had wanted to get that disciple, however, it would have devoured him during the night while he was asleep; and it would not have spared the donkey either. However, when God wanted to reveal the power of our holy Mother Walatta-Petros, he ordered the serpent to hiss and crawl about. For if the serpent had kept quiet, that disciple would not have noticed it. And if the disciple had not noticed it, who would have told us, and how would we have written down this miracle?

The disciple then traveled on in amazement and reached that settlement in Zhebey where Walatta-Petros lived in exile. He took the load from the donkey, went to our holy Mother Walatta-Petros, and, in front of her, put down the things that he had brought. Then, standing before her, he relayed a message from her mother and her brothers, reporting their greetings and warm wishes. Meanwhile, she looked him up and down, since she knew, before he revealed it to her, about the scare that he had received in the wilderness.

Therefore, she asked him, "Where did you spend last night, and what was the scare that you received?" She asked him as if she did not know.

[167]

He then told her everything that had happened.

She said, "Why were you afraid? Why were you terrified? Was not God with you? Does not scripture say, 'If God our Lord is with us, nobody can overcome us'? And does it not further say, 'Righteousness will surround you with a shield, and you will not be afraid of the dreadfulness of night. You will ride on the wolf and the serpent'? Therefore, do not be afraid of anything: Nothing will be able to harm you."

Chapter 33: More Disciples Join Our Mother in Zhebey

Then Walatta-Petros took the things—the garments and the gold that Takla-Maryam had brought—and gave some to the Black man every day, giving away her gifts in this way. When he then realized her supreme virtue, as well as the great grace and favor from God that rested upon her, he honored and cherished her very much and in the language of his region called her *Sitti*, which means "My Lady."

Indeed, God was with our holy Mother Walatta-Petros, just as the Torah says, "They threw Joseph into prison, the place where the prisoners live. He stayed there in prison, but God's help was with Joseph, and he poured out mercy and his love onto him. God gave Joseph favor and put clemency and compassion for him into the heart of the chief jailer. Therefore, the chief jailer appointed Joseph above all the prisoners because God was with Joseph and gave him success in everything he did." In addition, David says

in Psalms, "I was with him in the time of his trouble." Furthermore, our Lord says, "I will be with you every day until the end
of days."

[168]   Likewise, God was with our holy Mother Walatta-Petros and
showed her favor in front of the heathen Black man. At that time,
the Black man said to her, of his own volition and without anybody forcing him, "Everybody who wants to may come and live
with you. Even if there are many of them, even one hundred, I will
not be distressed and will not hinder them." Before this time,
though, when he had seen two or three people approaching, he
would chase them and want to kill them, but God would conceal
them from his eyes so that when he searched for them, he would
not find them.

Now, however, when he witnessed Walatta-Petros's supreme
virtue, as well as the great glory and favor from God that rested
upon her, he turned from evil toward goodness and allowed
Walatta-Petros's followers to stay. Thus, many persecuted Orthodox Christians came from all directions and gathered around her.
They surrounded her like bees gather around their king and surround him. Many were the men and women who formed a community with her in Zhebey. This was the first community.

Our holy Mother Walatta-Petros remained in Zhebey for three
years, overseeing them.

A captive also lived in Zhebey whose name was Ba-Haila-
Maryam. He was a monk whose feet had been put in heavy chains
because of his true faith—he was a truly righteous monk. He had
lived in that place before Walatta-Petros, but no one would visit
him. When our holy Mother Walatta-Petros noticed him, however,
she became very distressed and from then on assisted him and
provided him with food.

He then prophesied to her, "You will leave this place, but I will
die here. Yet, if I die while you are still here and if you bury me, I
know that God will have mercy on me on Judgment Day when he
will come to judge the world. Otherwise, though, it will not be; he
will not have mercy on me then."

Chapter 34: Our Mother Disobeys the King

After our holy mother had lived in Zhebey for three years, her brother Yohannes went to Fasiladas, son of the king and the future king, and beseeched him to speak to the king so that he would release our holy Mother Walatta-Petros from captivity. [169]

Yohannes said to Fasiladas, "Would it be right if she died in the land of pagans? She has been sick already, and death has just barely spared her. But such a thing must not be allowed to happen: mourning must not come between our two families."

So Fasiladas went to the king and spoke to him, "Order that Walatta-Petros be released from Zhebey so that she won't die there and so that her brothers won't one day become embittered against you. Truly, they love you and zealously support your rule."

The king replied, "Yes, I agree to your proposal. Let it be as you said."

Now the king dispatched one of his troops to the Black man to say to him, "Dismiss Walatta-Petros, whom I had ordered you to guard."

When the messenger arrived, he told the Black man the king's message, and he also told Walatta-Petros that the king said to her, "Depart!"

When the captive monk whom we mentioned before, Ba-Haila-Maryam, heard this, he became very sad and lost all hope. He said to himself, "Now I know that God will not have mercy on me." God was gracious toward him, however, and showed him his salvation and, before the multitudes, revealed his covenant with the righteous monk. Then the captive monk fell sick and said to our holy Mother Walatta-Petros, "How can you leave without burying me?"

She replied, "I will not leave without burying you!" So he rejoiced and kissed her hands.

Our holy Mother Walatta-Petros then asked the Black man to come up with an excuse and say to the king's messenger, "No written document of the king has reached me. You have lied to me—I will not dismiss her." The Black man said, "Very well," and did as she had told him.

Therefore, the messenger went away, returned to the king, and told him the response. The king instantly became enraged. Yet, he then wrote the document, the sign that was established between them, and dispatched that messenger again.

Meanwhile, the captive monk had died from his illness on the seventh day after the messenger's departure and thus found what he had desired. They buried him with chants and prayers, laying him in the tomb with his chains because they were so strong that they could not be unfastened. In this way, he consummated his good struggle and rested in peace, inheriting eternal life. May his prayers and blessing be with [manuscript owner's name] for eternity, amen.

[170]

Chapter 35: Our Mother Is Freed and Returns from Exile

After this, the king's messenger arrived again and gave the Black man the king's written message. The Black man received it and said, "The king's word is good."

Do you see, my loved ones, how an earthly king has no power and authority to kill anyone without the consent of God? Rather, God is the heavenly king, king of all flesh and spirit!

Many times King Susinyos had wanted to kill our holy Mother Walatta-Petros. Once, for instance, with the sword, when she stood before him and heaped abuse on him. But his counselors made him spare her, saying, "If you kill her, all her kin will be your enemies, the house of Dawaro and Fatagar."

Furthermore, Susinyos cleverly contrived a devilish stratagem to hide his wickedness, when he sent her to Zhebey. He ordered the Black man, "Build a hut for her as her dwelling place amid the grass of the wilderness, and then set the grass ablaze when the wind blows so that the fire will consume her and she will die. If you do this, I will reward you greatly."

So the Black man did as the king had ordered him and made our holy Mother Walatta-Petros live in a hut amid the grass—very high grass that he set ablaze at a distance. The fire burned down the grass, and its thundering sound could be heard from afar. Eventually, the fire reached the hut, rumbling like the thunder of the rainy season, and surrounded our holy Mother Walatta-Petros on every side, like a fence. Immediately, she prayed the prayer of the three biblical youths Shadrach, Meshach, and Abednego—"The fire and the flame praise God! He is glorified and exalted for eternity"— from its beginning to its end. She was not afraid, nor terrified at all, but rather eager to achieve death and collect the crown of martyrdom. Yet right away that fire went out; it was as if rain had fallen down on it. Thus, God demonstrated his power for her and saved her as he had saved the three youths.

[171]

She was not happy about her salvation, however, but instead sad because she desired death more than life, in keeping with what Paul says, "I desire to depart and separate from the world so that I can be with Christ. That would be much better and much more appropriate for me." However, God did not want our holy Mother Walatta-Petros to die but rather to live and tend his flock.

Therefore, when the king was incapable of killing her, he ordered that she be set free. Thus, the Black man said to her, "Depart and go forth, according to what the king has ordered."

So she departed and went forth, rejoicing in God, the father of mercy and Lord of all happiness. As the survivors of Babylon said, "When God revoked Zion's exile, we were overjoyed. Our mouths were filled with happiness and our tongues exulted."

Chapter 36: Our Mother Starts Her Second Community, at Chanqwa

With Walatta-Petros were Eheta-Kristos and Ilarya, as well as the disciples Takla-Maryam and Atsqa-Hawaryaat. Also, other exiled monks and nuns departed together with her. On her return journey, our holy Mother Walatta-Petros arrived at Chanqwa, in the region of Dembiya. There she stayed for a while because the king had allowed her to live where she wanted. Many of the persecuted—Orthodox men and women who had taken off their monastic caps, thereby posing as secular people, and who had been scattered throughout the regions—gathered around her. They became like sons and daughters to her so that the words of the psalm might be fulfilled that say, "In the place of your fathers, children have been born unto you, and you will establish them as messengers to all the world. They will remember your name for all eternity." Their number increased with each day.

They became a single community. This was the second community.

Chapter 37: Our Mother's Community Suffers a Violent Illness

While our holy Mother Walatta-Petros was there, a violent illness broke out and many of her community contracted it. For this reason, the people of the region of Chanqwa became afraid and began to grumble against them, saying, "These wandering strangers brought a violent illness upon us." Therefore, the local people refrained from approaching them and rather kept their distance.

As a result, our holy Mother Walatta-Petros said, "If we remain here, soon there will be not one person left to bury those who have died. The hyenas will tear our dead bodies to pieces. It would be better for us to seek refuge on Angaraa Island." That island was close to the region where they were.

Immediately, therefore, they set out and, carrying their sick, went to that island and lived there.

There was a young nun, a servant girl of Lebaseeta-Kristos. She was of good character: she served everyone without ever growing weary and without grumbling in the least, neither against those of low rank nor against those of high rank. Rather, she served everyone equally, without partiality. One day, while the girl recited the

[172]

[173]

Praise of Our Lady Mary for the day of Thursday, Eheta-Kristos summoned her and sent her on an errand. The girl embarked upon the task as ordered, carrying out her commission, and returned. The prayer was on her lips without ceasing. Eheta-Kristos then sent her on another errand. Again, she went with the prayer on her lips.

Then our Lady Mary appeared to the girl and said, "Are you weary and exhausted? Quickly finish this prayer that is on your lips, then I will relieve you of this wearying and exhausting labor and take you to eternal rest."

As soon as the girl had completed her prayer, she began to feel a little unwell, as if exhausted. She told Eheta-Kristos what our Lady Mary had said to her. Then she instantly passed away, and another girl from among the sick community members passed away together with her.

At that time, there was no man around who could dig the needed graves except Father Zikra-Maryam.

So our holy and chosen Mother Walatta-Petros became distressed and, addressing him politely, asked, "My brother, what shall we do? Who will dig the graves for us?"

He replied indignantly, however, "What do you want from me? [174] What are you saying to me? Do you expect *me* to dig them even though I don't know how and can't? You yourself get up, gird your loins, and dig! Was it not you who gathered and assembled all the people and brought this illness? Yet, who will now enter into your service? But you go and finish what you have begun!"

She politely implored him again, however. This time he got up, indignant and grumbling, and our holy Mother Walatta-Petros pointed out to him the place where he should dig. So he took a spade and shoved it into the ground with one angry thrust. Right away, a deep and spacious pit fell open, one that could hold many people! Nobody had known of that pit before; rather, it was revealed thanks to the prayers of our holy Mother Walatta-Petros. Then, into that pit, they put all those nuns, all together, who had passed away. After them, many other sisters passed away and were also put into that pit. They entered into the Kingdom of Heaven.

May their prayers and blessings be with [manuscript owner's name] for eternity, amen.

Chapter 38: Our Mother Looks for a New Place to Live

While our blessed Mother Walatta-Petros was there on Angaraa Island in Lake Tana, her brother Za-Dinghil sent her these words, "Live on my land, which lies near Enfraaz. It is really beautiful, with trees and water. It will be better for you to live there."

Upon hearing this, Walatta-Petros said, "May God's will be done," and she began exploring many places—monastic settlements as well as islands such as Daga and Tsana—for the best location for her to live. At that time, she placed crosses on the holy *tabot*, a representation of the Ark of the Covenant, and with great devotion prayed for three weeks so that God would reveal to her the place where she should live. She cast lots, and by the will of God, three times, each week, the lots came out in favor of the region of Dera.

[175]

After this, she sent these words to her husband Malkiya-Kristos: "On which of the islands near Dera will the king allow me to live? And may the king command that people there not argue with me about the faith and the Eucharist."

Malkiya-Kristos went to King Susinyos and asked him as requested.

The king replied, "Hereby, I grant her permission to live on Tsana Island, and no one shall harm her there!"

After this news, she broke camp, departed from Angaraa Island, and moved to Tsana Island. There she began to live in the deserted hut of a monk.

Chapter 39: Our Mother Sees the Icon of Saint Mary

At that time, she saw the church of Our Lady Mary's Resting Place of Tsana Island. Indeed, in the time of the Europeans, women could

enter there! In addition, she was shown its icon of our Lady Mary, [176]
one that was of the Egyptians, painted in gold. In it, the Holy Virgin was neither too light nor too dark but of medium complexion, like the people of Ethiopia.

Immediately, our holy and chosen Mother Walatta-Petros exclaimed, "This painting truly resembles our Lady Mary!"

So the women who were with her inquired, "When have you seen our Lady Mary?!"

Immediately she altered her story and kept them in the dark, replying modestly, "I have not seen her. What I said was, 'Does this icon of our Lady Mary resemble her?' No, I didn't say, 'I have seen her.' "

Our holy Mother Walatta-Petros then observed three fasts on Tsana Island; namely, those commemorating the Holy Family's stay in Qusqwaam in Egypt, as well as those of Advent and Lent.

Chapter 40: Our Mother Founds Her Third Community, on Mitsillé Island

Over time, our holy Mother Walatta-Petros made Tsana Island resemble a capital city, owing to the great number of people assembling around her. Therefore, she did not want to remain there. So [177]
she prayed to God to reveal a place to her where she could live in solitude.

Thereupon, an angel of God appeared to her and said, "Go to Mitsillé Island! Truly, that is your destined place."

Now our holy Mother Walatta-Petros sent these words to Malkiya-Kristos, "Intercede for me before the king so that he will allow me to live on Mitsillé Island: it is a place of tranquility and I prefer to live there."

So Malkiya-Kristos asked King Susinyos as requested, and the king replied, "Hereby, I allow her to live there."

As a result, our holy Mother Walatta-Petros went forth and proceeded to Mitsillé Island. As soon as she saw that island, she loved it very much. The people there selected a house for her to live in. They found her one whose owner had abandoned it: he had been sent into exile. Walatta-Petros took possession of it and lived there.

Then the abbot of the Mitsillé Island Monastery came to her, accompanied by monks who were of the faith of the Europeans, and said to her, "Who admitted you to our place? You who have rebelled against the king? If the king hears of this, he will flare up in anger against us and take vengeance upon us. Leave us in peace! Otherwise we will have to use force against you."

Our holy Mother Walatta-Petros replied to them politely, "But the king told me 'Live where you wish'! If you regard me as your enemy, however, I will leave you and abandon your monastery to you. But if I remain here, it will cause you no harm whatsoever."

As a result they left her alone and went away, since she had vanquished them by speaking politely, just as scripture says, "Do not vanquish evil with evil but vanquish evil through doing good." Furthermore, the Apostle Peter says, "For such is the will of God, that with your good deeds you tie the tongues of foolish men who do not know God."

[178]   Afterward, our holy Mother Walatta-Petros lived on Mitsillé Island in perfect tranquility. Many people, men and women, gathered around her and lived with her. Also Tsegga-Kristos of Amba Maryam Monastery was there. They became a community: it was the third community.

Chapter 41: Our Mother Is Persecuted by Duke Silla-Kristos

At that time, Duke Silla-Kristos, who ultimately died in the faith of the Europeans, heard that our Mother Walatta-Petros was on Mitsillé Island together with many people, and that she had refused the Eucharist when administered by its Catholic priests. He became enraged, roaring like a lion, and ranted against her. He demanded: "Can it be that a woman defeats me? I will go to her, chastise her with the whip, and strike her on her cheeks! I will make her profess the faith of the Europeans and take their Eucharist!"

When our holy Mother Walatta-Petros heard this, she left Mitsillé Island by night and, fleeing, arrived and hid at the monastic settlement of Qoratsa, where we currently find ourselves. From there, she stealthily went to the Saint Michael church and concealed herself in the vestry outside the church, staying there for a number of days. Meanwhile, Duke Silla-Kristos sallied forth but passed by in a boat without noticing her because God did not allow him to do her harm; thus, his plan failed abjectly. For the Psalter rightly says, "The Lord frustrates the plans of the princes." It was not for fear of flagellation or death that our holy Mother Walatta-Petros fled from Mitsillé Island but rather on account of the verse that says, "Do not put God your Lord to the test!"

[179]

Thereafter, our holy Mother Walatta-Petros returned to Mitsillé Island. Then people told her, "Mezraata-Kristos has come with a written authorization from the king to take captive the Christians in the entire region of Dera who have not embraced the faith of the Europeans, and he is also looking for you specifically. In fact, he is already here!"

When our holy Mother Walatta-Petros heard this, she again departed, fleeing to Sadachilla, which was safe. Later, she again returned to Mitsillé Island.

Furthermore, people relate, "She once was sent out onto Lake Tana all alone on a boat without a pole and without anyone accompanying her, while a violent wind was blowing, so that the waves would capsize her and make her drown, and she would die. Immediately though, the boat was lifted up from the lake and flew like an arrow flies, taking her to a port. Flying once again, it then took her back to her place of departure." Many from among the monastic brothers and sisters were witnesses to this miracle, and their testimonies agree.

After this, our holy Mother Walatta-Petros lived on Mitsillé Island in peace. With her were about fifty people in number. They lived in a single house, blessing the meal together and eating their food joyfully. The men and the women were not separated except for sleeping because there was no thought of sin in their hearts. They were all pure, as Walatta-Petros herself testified when she said, "The demon of fornication and the demon of desire are not permitted in my house!"

[180]   It is said of one of them, whose name was Marqoréwos, that he used to leap up into the air on wings and go to Zagé.

Chapter 42: King Susinyos Renounces the Filthy Faith of the Europeans

While our holy Mother Walatta-Petros lived on Mitsillé Island, there rose up a pretender to the throne whose name was Malkiya-Kristos; he declared himself king in the province of Lasta, to the east. Then Bihono and his army, who had been sent by Malkiya-Kristos, came and besieged King Susinyos. Malkiya-Kristos wanted to kill the king and seize his kingdom.

As a result, King Susinyos became frightened and terrified and made a vow, "If God gives me power and victory, and if he delivers this rebel into my hand, I will profess the faith of the Orthodox pope Dioscoros and renounce the filthy faith of the Catholic pope Leo."

[181]   Luckily for King Susinyos, things went as he had asked: he beat and killed Bihono and returned to his court in tranquility. After this, he sent around a herald who proclaimed, "Whosoever, after he has heard my word, disobeys my order, and professes the faith of the Europeans—may his house be pillaged and may he himself be punished with death. Those Christians who have been sent into exile, however, may each return to their provinces and private lands."

This was a great joy for the Christians: they returned to their homes praising God and thanking him. Then the king sent a message with the good news to our holy Mother Walatta-Petros: "Behold, I have reestablished the faith of the Christians and abolished the faith of the Europeans! Rejoice and exult! May there be peace between you and me from now on."

Chapter 43: Our Mother Celebrates the Return of the True Faith

When the king's messenger arrived at our holy Mother Walatta-Petros's home on Mitsillé Island, he gave her the written message that said this. She received it, read it, and was happy, shouting with joy, just as the Psalter says, "You peoples all clap your hands and celebrate before God with joyful voices!" Also, the priests who were with her sang, "We praise God the praiseworthy to whom praise is due!" That day was July 7.

The next day the king's messenger said to our holy Mother Walatta-Petros, "Grant me leave to go to Tsana Island because the king has ordered me to take the good news there, too."

Accordingly, our holy Mother Walatta-Petros instructed Father [182] Za-Sillasé, "Take this messenger to Tsana Island. Also, catch some fish for me there so that I can serve them in a stew for the Feast of Peter and Paul."

He responded, "Very well."

So she blessed Father Za-Sillasé and dismissed him. He left with the king's messenger and took him to Tsana Island. Right after this, Father Za-Sillasé dropped his nets, throwing them into the lake, and was lucky enough to catch fish. He spent the entire day fishing and then returned to Mitsillé Island, coming with a catch of thirteen fish.

These he presented to our holy Mother Walatta-Petros, saying, "Look, now I bring you what God has given me through your blessing."

Our holy Mother Walatta-Petros responded, "These twelve fish are like the apostles, but this one is like their master, Christ. May the blessings of the apostles and the blessing of their master, Christ, rest upon you!"

"Amen!" Father Za-Sillasé replied.

This thing that happened was truly miraculous, that the quantity of fish neither exceeded nor fell short of this number. On the next day was the Feast of Paul and Peter. Walatta-Petros had a stew prepared from those fish and fed her entire community and all the people of the monastery.

Chapter 44: King Susinyos Dies and Our Mother Remains on Mitsillé Island

After this had happened in July, King Susinyos died on September 17, 1632, on Our Lady's Feast of Tsédénya. In his stead, his son

[183]

Fasiladas became king; he fully restored the Orthodox faith. Father Atsfa-Kristos, the rightful abbot of Mitsillé Island Monastery, who had been a captive in the town of Téra, returned in those days, and also other monks who had been exiled or who had fled from the religion of the Europeans.

After this our holy Mother Walatta-Petros remained on Mitsillé Island for a full year because she had made a vow to Saint Fasiladas with the following words, "If the Orthodox faith is reestablished, I will remain for another year, and I will receive the Eucharist in this church of yours."

Thus, she remained on Mitsillé Island, receiving the Eucharist from the hands of formerly exiled priests. Every time during Communion that a priest said, "Send the grace of the Holy Spirit," she would plainly see the descent of the Holy Spirit. Also, when evening fell each day, she would enter the church and stand like a fixed pillar before the icon of our Lady Mary, without leaning against a wall or a column. She would pray and plead for the salvation of her soul and the deliverance of all the people. She would spend the entire night praying, without rest. Then, when morning

[184]

came and the sun rose, when the *Lives of the Saints* was read, and when the closing prayer was finished, she would leave the church and go to her home. There she would read the Gospel of John. She would do this every day, becoming like Father Arsenius. The number of her years in that year was thirty-nine.

Chapter 45: Our Mother Is Healed
of an Abundant Flow of Blood

At that time, an abundant flow of menstrual blood used to torment Walatta-Petros, and she suffered greatly. During her standing at night in the church, she would implore the icon of our Lady Mary, saying to her, "I beg you, my Lady, for my sake, implore the Lord that this blood may dry up! I am truly tormented."

One night, the icon then spoke to her and said, "Why do you constantly importune me? Behold, I have heard your prayers and have seen your suffering! For your sake, I now dry up your period. From now on, therefore, blood will never again flow from you."

Right away, then, her period dried up, even though she was still young and had not yet reached the age at which menstruation ceases. She resembled the woman who had touched the hem of the Lord Jesus's clothes, in keeping with what Jesus had said to her, [185] "Your faith has healed you." Likewise, full of faith, our holy Mother Walatta-Petros had stood before the icon of our Lady Mary and was healed from this illness.

As for the former exiles, they used to visit our holy Mother Walatta-Petros every day and exchange stories of all the tribulations and hardships that each had encountered in exile. But they also rejoiced over their return and spoke among themselves just as Paul had spoken, "Now indeed that life of ours for which we had hoped is near. The night has passed and the day has come."

Furthermore, they said, "Blessed be our Lord God who did not deliver us into the treacherous net of the Europeans! Indeed, our souls fled like birds from a hunting net. Now, the net has been torn asunder, and we are safe."

Chapter 46: Our Mother Is Challenged by a Monk

In those days, our holy Mother Walatta-Petros celebrated the memorial service of our Father Zara-Yohannes because he had died at

Amba Maryam Monastery (from which he previously had been exiled). She generously gave much to eat and drink to the people of the Mitsillé Island Monastery and to the entire community. She exhausted everything she had and did not save anything for the next day, according to what the Gospel says, "Do not say: 'This is for the next day,' because the next day will itself take care of itself."

[186]   Yet one monk grumbled when he saw this, "What is this giving without restraint while we don't have our daily bread? Is this not being done for empty praise? But what will *we* eat tomorrow?!"

Eheta-Kristos rebuked him, however, "O you of poor understanding and lacking in hope! Do you imagine God is as poor as yourself? Is he not so rich that he can satisfy whoever calls out to him, today just as much as tomorrow?"

At that very moment, messengers arrived with food about which no one had had any prior knowledge, nine donkey loads here and four donkey loads there. Those who witnessed it marveled and praised God.

Chapter 47: Our Mother Establishes Her Fourth Community, at Zagé

One full year after the days of persecution were over, Walatta-Petros again prayed for three weeks with great devotion, standing before that icon of Saint Mary, which previously had spoken to her. Walatta-Petros said to Saint Mary, "My Lady, I implore you to reveal to me the place where I should live and to enlighten me as to your will and the will of your son."

So the icon once again spoke to our holy Mother Walatta-Petros and said to her, "Go to Zagé! Truly, this is my wish, and the wish of my beloved son."

After Walatta-Petros had heard this pronouncement from the icon of our Lady Mary, she assembled Father Atsfa-Kristos, abbot of the Mitsillé Island Monastery, and the monks. She bid them farewell and told them that she would go to Zagé. In addition, she implored them not to bring anything female onto Mitsillé Island because in the hagiography of our Father Afqaranna-Egzee, who lived three hundred years before, she had found the prohibition that no female creature, human or animal, should set foot on the island.

They replied, "So be it!" and on that very day they expelled the female creatures who were on Mitsillé Island. Father Atsfa-Kristos furthermore forbade female creatures from ever being readmitted to Mitsillé Island. [187]

Our holy Mother Walatta-Petros took her leave from them after she had established this rule. She left that day and spent the night at Owf Gojjo. From there, she departed and arrived at the monastic settlement of Zagé.

There she remained, and many people gathered around her, grown men as well as grown women, old folks as well as children, young men as well as young women. They came from east and west, with their number increasing by the day. This was the fourth community.

Chapter 48: Zagé Male Leaders Work against Our Mother

Then Satan entered into the hearts of important men of the previously established Zagé community and roused them against Walatta-Petros. They went to her with their spiritual leader and said to her, "Who brought you here, and who has given this monastic settlement to you? Is it not ours? So, now we say to you, 'Leave, in peace!' or else we will use force with you and set your hut on fire."

Our holy Mother Walatta-Petros received them with love and courtesy, however, and served them food and drink. They ate their fill and came to their senses. They returned to goodness, left her in peace, and went away. Truly, scripture says likewise, "If your enemy is hungry, feed him, if he is thirsty, give him something to drink. If you do this, you will heap burning coals upon his head."

[188]

At that time, after having heard of this, Father Tsawaaré-Masqal, the abbot of Tsana Island Monastery, and Father Mankir of Wonchet Monastery came to visit our holy Mother Walatta-Petros. She told them what the important men had said to her.

Upon hearing this, Father Tsawaaré-Masqal replied, "Don't be distressed. If you want to live at Zagé, no one can hinder you. Let us send a message to the king, and he will announce this monastic settlement as your place of residence. Or else, live in the monastic settlement of Qoratsa; I myself will grant it to you. However, first, give us your okay.

"For now, we would like to suggest one other thing: Come and let us go to Béta Manzo. We would like to spend some time there with you so that Tsegga-Kristos might interpret the *Comprehensive Book* for us."

Chapter 49: Our Mother Escapes an Epidemic

With difficulty, they managed to get her to consent to leave Zagé. But this departure was due to God's wise foresight because he wanted to protect her from an epidemic. Also, other religious people who possessed foreknowledge informed her, "Behold, an epidemic will come and kill many of your followers. You should depart so that you may survive and later again be an example for everyone."

[189]

Some people even say, "The epidemic revealed itself to her while bending its bow." So they urged her, "Depart!"

So our holy Mother Walatta-Petros went with Father Tsawaaré-Masqal and Father Mankir, came to Béta Manzo, and stayed there. After this a man, the father of Kristos-Sinnaa, came to Zagé, where Walatta-Petros's community welcomed him. But on that same day, he began to suffer from the epidemic's illness, and died on the third day. In those days, many monks and nuns fell ill due to that epidemic.

When our holy Mother Walatta-Petros heard of this, she said, "I, too, will go and die together with my disciples. I want to share in their illness and in every tribulation that befalls them."

But they implored her and forbade her to go; they said to her, "If you went and died together with them, that would not benefit them in any way. Rather, we will send people who can carry away the sick and bury the dead."

With difficulty, they made Walatta-Petros give up the idea of returning to Zagé. Then they dispatched people there, as they had promised. During that period, fifty-seven souls died from the epidemic. They completed their earthly struggle and entered the Kingdom of Heaven, gaining what God had also solemnly promised to our father Saint Takla-Haymanot four hundred years before, saying to him, "If your followers die of an epidemic, I will count them among the martyrs and I will entrust them to you in the Kingdom of Heaven." May their prayers and blessings be with [manuscript owner's name] for eternity, amen.

Chapter 50: The Mother of Our Mother Dies

So our holy Mother Walatta-Petros remained in Béta Manzo. There she began to restore the church, which had gone to ruin. At that time, her mother Kristos-Ebayaa arrived because she wanted to visit our holy Mother Walatta-Petros. At Béta Manzo, Kristos-Ebayaa fell ill by the will of God. When the illness violently seized her and she was close to death, Walatta-Petros ordered her to be taken to Réma Island Monastery, but she died while she was still [190] on the boat, before arriving on the island. Then she was buried on Réma Island. Meanwhile, our holy Mother Walatta-Petros was at Béta Manzo, where she heard the news and wept for her mother.

As for the church of Béta Manzo, it was rebuilt through the will of God, with Walatta-Petros drawing water and carrying stones for the construction. Afterward, she sent people with boats to pick up the surviving sick from Zagé. They went and took them to a little island that was close to Gwangoot until they had fully recovered. After this, our holy Mother Walatta-Petros went to Réma Island Monastery to hold the memorial service for her mother. There she performed the memorial services of the thirtieth and the fortieth day. After this, the months of the rainy season began.

Chapter 51: Our Mother Raises the
Monk Silla-Kristos from the Dead

Walatta-Petros spent the rainy season on Réma Island and while there worked a miracle: she resuscitated Silla-Kristos after he had died, as he himself has testified.

One day, while Réma Island Monastery lacked a deacon who could celebrate the Liturgy—because the Europeans had contaminated the deacons with Catholicism and a new patriarch who could ordain deacons had not yet arrived from Egypt—our holy Mother Walatta-Petros ordered Silla-Kristos to celebrate the Liturgy, but he replied, "No!"

So she ordered him again, but he again replied, "No!" Thereby, he aggrieved her.

Furthermore, he disdained her and held her in contempt, saying in his heart, but not with his mouth, "What is it with this woman who gives me orders, acting as if she were a spiritual leader or a monastic superior? Does not scripture say to her, 'We do not allow a woman to teach, nor may she exercise authority over a man'?"

[191] Our holy Mother Walatta-Petros was aware of his concealed thoughts but did not reveal anything to him. In that month, on September 18, was the Feast of Saint Fasiladas. For this reason, Silla-Kristos went to Mitsillé Island. But when God wanted to reveal the power of our holy Mother Walatta-Petros, he brought down a severe disease on Silla-Kristos, who fell sick on the very day that he had left Réma Island.

When the disease began to affect him badly, he said, "Take me to Réma," and right away, he was picked up and taken there. He was laid down in Tabota-Kristos's house. He already was like a corpse. He did not eat, he did not drink, he did not move, and he did not speak. Rather, the whole day he groaned, "My God! My God!" His entire body swelled: he was afflicted with dropsy.

On the eighth day after he had fallen sick, Silla-Kristos died on the Feast of Father Ewostatéwos, the holy monk of old, on September 25. Then water was heated to wash him, a cloth was brought to shroud him, and his dead body was wrapped in it. The threads of the shrouding cloth were carefully tied together, and everything one does for a dead body was properly performed. Then messengers went and told our holy Mother Walatta-Petros about Silla-Kristos's passing. They found her reading the book of the *Miracles of Our Lady Mary*, and told her that he had died.

Instantly, she went to the church, taking that book with her. [192] Then she stood before the icon of our Lady Mary and implored her, "My Lady, it shouldn't be like this! Truly, I didn't ask you to kill him but to chasten him. The chastening that he received through his disease suffices as punishment for him. Merciful One, have mercy for my sake!"

Now fingers emerged from the *Miracles* book and tapped on Walatta-Petros's mouth. In addition, a voice emanated from inside the icon and said to her, "You of two tongues, go away! I hereby grant you the mercy you have asked for."

Immediately our holy Mother Walatta-Petros left the church, returned to her home, summoned Eheta-Kristos, and said to her, "Has Silla-Kristos died before turning himself into a monk? I beg you, go to him, call out his name three times, and say to him, 'Silla-Kristos, turn yourself into a monk!'"

Eheta-Kristos went to him, called out his name three times, and said to him, "Silla-Kristos, turn yourself into a monk!"

Instantly, he woke up, opened his eyes, looked at her, and heard the words that she had addressed to him. With his eyes, he then made a sign to her as if saying "Yes!"

Now they brought a monk's cap, blessed it for him, and put it on his head. At that moment, he rose up and was alive again, like before. Then they brought him food, and he ate.

Chapter 52: The Monk Silla-Kristos Sees a Vision

Listen further: We will tell you about the vision that Silla-Kristos saw on the day that his soul separated from his body. He recounted, "A man of light with the appearance of a monk came to me. It seemed to me that he was Father Ewostatéwos; the day, in fact, was that of his feast. This man took me with him, making me ascend up high and showing me a luminous and bright town whose colors are unknown in this world and whose shapes are inexpressible in earthly terms. Beyond that town, he furthermore showed me another one that was called Paradise. In that town were big trees without fruit, but also small trees with fruit. So, I asked the man, 'What are these big trees that bear no fruit?' The man responded, 'They are monks who thought highly of themselves. They went by the name of monks, wore the clothes of monks, and wanted to be called "Father" here and "Father" there, but they did not do the work of monks. Rather, they spent their days in laziness and sloth, constantly wandering from town to town. Therefore, they did not bring forth any fruitful works.' I then further asked him, 'So, those small trees that bear fruit, what are they?' and he further replied, 'They are monks who humbled themselves, who were not famous and whom nobody knew except God. They stayed awake day and night in prayer and in prostration, wandering to minister for the relief of others. Therefore, they brought forth abundant fruit, as the Gospel says in the Parable of the Seed, "There is some seed that falls between the thorns, and the thorns suffocate and choke it so that it does not bear fruit. But there is also some seed that falls on good soil and yields fruit, some hundredfold, some sixtyfold, and some thirtyfold." ' "

[194]

Silla-Kristos told us all these things: that Walatta-Petros had killed him, that she had resuscitated him, and that he had seen this vision. He is alive right up to now, and his testimony is trustworthy; he does not lie.

Do you see the great power of our holy Mother Walatta-Petros, how she made him who covertly had spoken ill of her and abused her, fall ill and die? She, too, covertly killed him and covertly resuscitated him. That is, she did not say to him, "Rise up!" but rather said to him, "Turn yourself into a monk!" because she feared vain praise. Saying "Turn yourself into a monk," however, amounts to saying, "Rise up!" She herself told him this, saying, "I killed you and I resuscitated you through the power of my Lord. For you had treated me with contempt and abused me."

So it is not acceptable for people to speak ill of and abuse those whom God has set up as leaders and appointed, in keeping with what scripture says: "Do not speak ill of your people's leader." In the past, when Miriam and Aaron had secretly spoken ill of and abused Moses, leprosy sores had appeared on Miriam and she had been expelled from the camp of the Israelites for seven days until [195] they had confessed with their mouths and openly declared their sins, with Aaron saying to Moses, "We have sinned because we have spoken ill of God. Please, pray for her so that this leprosy disappears from her." So Moses prayed for Miriam, and she was healed. This story of Silla-Kristos is similar.

Chapter 53: Our Mother Saves Her Followers from an Epidemic

After this incident, our holy Mother Walatta-Petros went forth and proceeded to Damboza Island. She remained there for some time. But on Damboza Island, too, a grave disease broke out from which the entire community fell sick. Twelve souls from among them who had survived the earlier epidemic died. They completed their earthly struggle and passed away in peace, inheriting eternal life. May their prayers and blessings be with [manuscript owner's name], for eternity, amen.

Those who survived suffered great torment, such that their bodies were covered with scabs and their entire appearance changed by the ferocity of the disease and by hunger.

In those days, the new Ethiopian Orthodox patriarch, our Father Marqos, arrived from Egypt; he had reached the district of Walwaj. Therefore, the leaders of the local church sent a message to Walatta-Petros and informed her about the patriarch's arrival. They said to [196] her, "Come and let us go to the patriarch in order to welcome him, ask to be blessed by him, and then receive his blessing."

When our holy Mother Walatta-Petros heard this, she felt greatly distressed and said to herself, "If I go forth alone and leave these sick disciples behind on Damboza Island, they will die of hunger. I will then have nobody to follow me as my disciples. But if I make them follow me now, they will not be able to walk. Then again, if I desist from going, I will be deprived of the patriarch's blessing." She was at a loss about what to do. This took place in January. While our holy Mother Walatta-Petros found herself thus between two thoughts, she prayed to God so that he might reveal to her which of the two courses of action he wanted and would be pleased with.

Now a word came from heaven, "Order all the sick ones to go down to Lake Tana on the festival day celebrating Christ's baptism: the Holy Spirit will then descend on them and they will be cured of their illness."

So when the day of celebration came, Walatta-Petros took her sick followers down to the lake, and they all performed the ritual immersion. The Holy Spirit then descended upon them, just as it had once descended at the fortress of Zion in the guise of fire. Directly, all the sick were cured that day, becoming as though the illness had never touched them at all. All those present at the place of celebration saw this and marveled at it.

Chapter 54: Our Mother Is Blessed by the Egyptian Patriarch

Now our holy Mother Walatta-Petros set out and joyfully traveled to see the patriarch. As for him, he had been informed about her entire story before she met him—how, for instance, she had separated from her husband Malkiya-Kristos because he had the garments of our Father Simeon, the murdered former patriarch. He further had been told, "Behold, Walatta-Petros is on her way." He then waited until she arrived. When our holy Mother Walatta-Petros arrived, she greeted the patriarch respectfully.

[197]

When the new patriarch, our Father Marqos, saw her, he inquired of his retinue, "Is this the one whose fame has reached our land, the land of Egypt?"

They replied, "Yes, that's her."

So he blessed her with a blessing appropriate for a person of her spiritual achievements and loved her very much. She now told him what was foremost on her mind, saying to him, "What am I to do? Behold, people assemble around me even though I don't want that. Do I have to accept it or not?"

The patriarch replied, "Don't be afraid of anything! Nothing happens but by the will of God. May he now therefore strengthen you, and may he let his Spirit rest upon you." He then conferred the priesthood upon the men who were with her. Thereafter, they took their leave of each other: the patriarch proceeded on his way to the king, while Walatta-Petros returned the way she had come.

Chapter 55: Our Mother's Community Flees a Leopard at Zagé

In the meantime, many people, men and women with their sons and daughters, had joined Walatta-Petros's community on Damboza Island; they had become very numerous indeed. Shortly afterward, Walatta-Petros arrived back on Damboza Island. When she saw how numerous the people there had become, she realized [198] that no place other than Zagé would be able to hold them. Therefore, she again wanted to live at Zagé.

However, she first went to Béta Manzo, where she began a fast. She continued it until the Feast of the Mount of Olives. She also completed the reconstruction of the church at Béta Manzo that she had previously begun.

After that, she moved to Zagé. Then the feast of Easter came, the feast of our Lord's resurrection. On that very night, while our holy Mother Walatta-Petros kept praying after all the others had fallen asleep—while her eyes remained open—she was struck by a drowsiness, as in a vision. Then she heard a voice tell her, "Say 'Deliver me from blood, God, Lord of my Salvation!' "

She regarded this as a dream, however, and returned to her earlier prayer. But again, a drowsiness struck her, like before, and again she heard something, as if a voice were saying the same thing to her. Then again, for a third time, it said to her, "Say 'Deliver me from blood, God, Lord of my Salvation!' "

Now our holy Mother Walatta-Petros pondered, asking herself, "What does this vision mean?" At that moment, she perceived the shadow of a leopard, creeping along, outside in the moonlight. Sometimes it would pause, wanting to surge forth, sometimes it would crouch on the ground, lying in wait and ready to attack. She did not realize, however, that it was a real leopard. Then, while our holy Mother Walatta-Petros marveled at the vision, the leopard surged forth and snatched a little boy who was sleeping in the compound. Now our holy Mother Walatta-Petros saw the leopard as it went away.

[199]   At that time, none of the sisters except for her had perceived the leopard, which had taken the child away and hid him. Then the leopard came again and snatched a little girl who was sleeping. It seized her by the sole of her foot and, dragging her, pulled her outside. The little girl screamed while the leopard dragged her, and all the sisters who had been sleeping immediately woke up and saw the leopard dragging the little girl, tossing her around on the ground and amusing itself with her.

Afraid and terrified, they all fled toward our holy Mother Walatta-Petros, seeking refuge with her, falling all over her and squeezing against her until she almost died. Meanwhile, the leopard kept amusing itself with the screaming little girl outside. Truly, the leopard had been ordered by God to scare and terrify them. After this, it went away. As for the boy child the leopard had snatched first, it had eaten into his body and then buried him in the ground, left him, and then gone back to snatch the girl.

The sisters spent the entire night agitated and terrified. When morning came, they remembered the little boy. They searched for him, but did not find him, and realized that the leopard had snatched him at night. Now all the monks gathered and searched for those children's dead bodies. With difficulty, they found the boy, and they buried him. But the girl remained missing.

On that day, great terror and tumult reigned in the entire community. They unanimously said to our holy Mother Walatta-Petros, "Let's leave! Fear and terror of that leopard's great, awe-inspiring power have us in their grip. We don't have it in us to remain in this wild place." Others said to her, "Leave and don't oppose God! Don't be like someone who fights with God."

She agreed and went along with them in this decision. She allowed the healthy to leave on foot and the sick by boat. On that very day, they left Zagé and went to Furé. Our holy Mother Walatta-Petros left with the sick ones. Then, the healthy ones departed on foot, whereas she had left by boat together with the ill and weak ones. They all met again on Damboza Island.

My loved ones, please do not think that our holy Mother Walatta-Petros fled for fear of that leopard or because she was horrified by death. Rather, it was because of the fear of the sisters, her daughters. As scripture says, "Truly, if one member suffers, our entire body suffers with it." As for her, she understood perfectly well that she could not escape God's will by running away. As David says in Psalms, "Where can I go from your Spirit, and where can I flee from your face? If I ascended into the sky, you would be there too, and if I descended into the abyss, you would be there also. If I took wings like an eagle and flew to the end of the ocean, there also your hand would guide me, and your right hand would hold me." [200]

Now, regarding those children whom the leopard had snatched, God authorized and allowed it to take them, according to what David says in Psalms, "The flesh of your righteous ones is for the animals of the wilderness."

Chapter 56: Our Mother Founds Her Fifth Community, on Damboza Island

After that, our holy and blessed Mother Walatta-Petros had people construct a large communal building on Damboza Island. She lived there with her daughters, the nuns. As for the monks, they lived on Tsana Island nearby. On Damboza Island, too, many people, men and women, gathered around her, like vultures gather around carcasses. They grew numerous; their number increased with each [201] day, just as it says in the Acts of the Apostles. At that time, Father Za-Hawaryaat and Father Eda-Kristos arrived at her community. This was the fifth community.

Then a severe disease broke out, and many monks and nuns fell ill. During that period, eighty-seven souls died. They completed their earthly course, passed away in peace, and inherited eternal life. May their prayers and blessings be with [manuscript owner's name] for eternity, amen.

Chapter 57: Why Our Mother Prayed for the Faithful to Die

But there were also those who recovered from that illness. They are alive today and witness regarding Walatta-Petros. They report, "When our holy Mother Walatta-Petros said to us, 'If at this moment I so desired, you would be shot with guns, or pierced with spears,' we immediately fell sick and almost died. Furthermore, when she watched over us and sent us the following message, 'May God have mercy on you and heal you!,' we responded, 'If *you* have mercy on us, God too will be willing to show us mercy.' So then she asked us, 'Do you really want to live?' We replied, 'Yes indeed, we want to live!' She responded, 'Don't be afraid, you will not die.' Then she swore the customary oath. Now we were happy because she had let us know our fate in no uncertain terms. Immediately then, we recovered and could stand up again."

[202] This testimony is trustworthy and no lie. It is just as the Apostle James says in the Bible, "The prayer of a righteous one helps greatly. It is powerful, and it confers power. Elijah was a man like us, and like we suffer, he suffered. Yet, he prayed that it might not rain, and for three years and six months it did not rain on the

earth. Then he prayed again that it might rain, and, accordingly, the sky released its rain and the earth let sprout its fruits." In this manner, God obeys his saints, listens to their prayers, and does for them all they desire.

When our holy Mother Walatta-Petros came to understand her disciples' thinking but also realized what awaited them on Judgment Day, she asked God in prayer that the sick might immediately die in their flesh but live with their souls in eternal life, which never ceases. As David says in Psalms about the Lord, "Truly, your mercy is better than living," and Paul furthermore says, "As you believers have assembled in the name of our Lord Jesus Christ, hand that man over to Satan so that his flesh be destroyed but his spirit saved on the Day of our Lord Jesus Christ."

For this reason, our holy Mother Walatta-Petros would not spare anybody regarding death in the flesh, since the secrets of everyone lay open to her, and she had insight into each person's character. As Paul says, "He who has the Holy Spirit scrutinizes everything. Him, however, nobody can scrutinize." And truly, the Holy Spirit rested on our holy Mother Walatta-Petros: She knew what would happen before it happened, be it good or bad; she examined everyone's heart and innermost feelings, had insight into people's thoughts, and told them those thoughts before they expressed them to her. Therefore, nobody would approach her without examining and scrutinizing themselves. Just as that which is poured into a glass cup, be it scant or abundant, is visible, so the thoughts that were in the hearts of men were visible to her. [203]

Because of this ability, she did not desire that anyone should perish forever, but rather implored God, and he would do for her everything she desired. He would bring illness and thereby kill, according to what she had asked from him because he had promised her to do so when he had granted her the protective promise in Waldeba. Our holy Mother Walatta-Petros always did as follows: When she saw people from her community producing numerous and abundant good works, she implored God for their death and dispatched them to God as a gift, just as a farmer watches and looks at his field, how it ripens and becomes ready for the harvest, and then assembles the harvesters, dispatches them to harvest for him, and collects his grain into his granaries.

[204]

Chapter 58: Our Mother Orders the
Separation of Monks and Nuns

Furthermore, when the monks and the nuns had become numerous, Walatta-Petros established among them a rule: that they should not talk and flirt with each other, neither while walking nor standing nor sitting, so that Satan would not assault them, nor sow weeds in their hearts, thereby spoiling the seeds of righteousness that had been sown into their hearts, just as the Gospel relates in the Parable of the Seed.

My loved ones, please do not think that our holy Mother Walatta-Petros established a peculiar rule. Rather, the 318 Bishops of the Council of Nicaea had already established it, saying, "More than anything else, the righteous ones and the monks must stay away from women. They must not respond to them, and definitely must not actively engage them in conversation." Therefore, for us it is also righteous and proper to follow this rule and place it like a ring on our heart or like a seal tattooed on our arm. As Paul says, "If our fathers who have begotten us in the flesh discipline us and we respect them, how much more should we not then humble ourselves before the Father of our spirit and obey him, so that we may live? They, our fathers in the flesh, for our benefit disciplined us for a short time as they thought best, whereas he, God, disciplines us for our sake so that we may obtain his sanctification." In the moment when it is meted out each reprimand does not feel like a pleasure but like an affliction. Later though, its fruit is peace for those who have been reprimanded, and it earns them righteousness.

[205]

This is why our holy Mother Walatta-Petros said, "If with my own eyes I should see a monk and a nun talking and flirting with each other, I would want to jointly pierce them through, both of them, with a spear. I would not be worried that my doing this would be considered a crime, for just like the biblical priest Phinehas killed Zimri and the Midianite woman, and just like Samuel killed Agag—even though Phinehas and Samuel were priests who were not allowed to kill—they were moved by great zeal for God, so it was not a crime for them. Rather, God said to them, 'You have given my heart relief.'"

Furthermore, if our holy Mother Walatta-Petros was informed that a monk and a nun had violated this rule, she would suffer exceedingly. She would moan and roll around on the ground, until she was vomiting, as well as urinating blood and pus.

Chapter 59: Our Mother Suffers a Secret Affliction [206]

Walatta-Petros also suffered continuously from a subtle affliction that was invisible to the eyes of others. Due to this condition, she can be counted among the martyrs, according to what she herself testified when the sisters asked her, "Our Mother, everything that the prophets, apostles, and saints have spoken has been fulfilled in due time. Can it be that the words of the saints regarding you should be false? Namely, we have heard that you are destined to become a martyr."

Our holy Mother Walatta-Petros replied to them, "I have no idea. I don't know if God, for my sake, would consider the suffering that, hidden from you, I endure on a daily basis to be like the suffering of the martyrs." This is why our holy Mother Walatta-Petros spent many days afflicted by that kind of suffering, or by a similar one, when she saw or heard that members of her community had transgressed the spiritual statute that she had imposed on them. She did not leave them to be tormented by the afflictions they brought upon themselves; rather, she would suffer on their behalf and would offer herself up as a ransom for their souls, just as Paul says, "Who is it who suffers even though he is not sick? Me. And who is it who laughs and is not scared?" He furthermore says, "In truth I say to you, in Christ—I do not lie and my witness is the Holy Spirit who is in my heart—that my heart constantly grieves and suffers for them, such that I desire to be separated from Christ for the sake of my brothers and my kin."

[207]   Our holy Mother Walatta-Petros emulated Paul and always was worried that she would be held responsible for the souls of her disciples, according to what the Gospel says, "Truly, to whom great authority has been given, of him much will be asked; and to whom much has been entrusted, he will be thoroughly scrutinized." Therefore, if our holy Mother Walatta-Petros was sick and suffered for our sake to this extent, it is then necessary that we scrupulously observe her rules, as well as carry out her commandments carefully and diligently, and not eat from the forbidden tree like Adam and Eve, so as not to be chased from paradise. Let us not, like Achan, steal what God has forbidden, so as not to bring death upon ourselves—not only the death of the body but the death of the soul.

Chapter 60: Our Mother Repairs the Church on Réma Island

But let us return to our previous narration. Our holy Mother Walatta-Petros was living on Damboza Island in a way similar to Paul, in the communal building that she had ordered to be built, near the church whose tabot, the representation of the Ark of the Covenant, was dedicated to Saint Mary of Qusqwaam. There, each day, she would spend much of the night and the early morning hours imploring and supplicating our Lady Mary and her beloved Son for the salvation of her soul, and particularly for the souls of all the members of her community.

Then Father Za-Maryam, the abbot of Réma Island Monastery, arrived on Damboza Island with many monks. They implored
[208]   Walatta-Petros to renovate their church for them, which was dedicated to the Savior of the World, and in which Walatta-Petros's father and mother lay buried.

She replied to them, "How could I, of all people, be capable of carrying out such a great task? However, let us pray to God, you and me, and then what he wills may happen." With these words, she granted them their leave. Thus, the monks turned back, returning to their monastery.

So our holy Mother Walatta-Petros prayed with great devotion for seven days in the church of Damboza Island, and our Lord revealed to her, "Go and build! I will be with you and assist you, and I will see to it that you complete the task."

After this, our blessed Mother Walatta-Petros left Damboza Island and went to Réma Island, accompanied by all the monks and nuns. She tore down the roof of the earlier large rectangular church and began building a beautiful structure, herself contributing by drawing water from Lake Tana and carrying it in a vessel on her back.

Many women of high rank—daughters of princesses, concubines of the king, and the wives of great lords—were with Walatta-Petros and took part in this work together with her, following her. On one occasion, they would draw water, on another carry mud and stones. There also were many monks.

Chapter 61: Our Mother Founds Her Sixth Community, at Afer Faras

Furthermore, in her community, there were those who had left father and mother, or wife and children, or all their possessions and fields, while others had sacrificed their youth and all their [209] carnal desires. There also were women who had left their husbands, and teenage girls who had preserved their virginity and betrothed themselves to their groom, Christ. They loved him dearly and followed him every day of their lives, just as Solomon says in the Song of Songs, "The maidens have loved you and have followed you." Further, there were children, boys and girls, who had followed their fathers and mothers. There were manservants and maidservants who had followed their masters, thereby liberating themselves from servitude, freeing themselves from subjection and becoming equal with their masters. In this way, they found rest from their difficult toil and labor, just as the Gospel says, "Come to me, you who are weary and carry a heavy load, and I will give you rest."

There were sinners and fornicators who had turned toward repentance, abandoning their former conduct and becoming chaste for Christ. And, finally, there were poor and wretched folks, the blind and the lame, who had entrusted themselves to Walatta-Petros and found refuge with her.

She opened the door to her house to anyone who wanted to enter, just as the Gospel says, "I will not chase away or expel anyone who comes to me." And as Paul says, "There is neither Jew nor heathen, and there is neither slave nor free." In those days, peace and love reigned. Nobody sought his own advantage but rather that of his neighbor. There were no strangers there and no kin; rather, all were equal, of a single heart and of a single soul while Christ was in their midst.

When the community became very numerous, however, Réma Island became too small for them and could not hold them anymore. Truly, their number increased with each day! Walatta-Petros then received a plot of land on the lakeshore that was called Afer Faras. This was the sixth community.

[210]

At Afer Faras, she built a house for herself and the sisters, while the brothers lived in the compound of the Afer Faras Church of Saint John. Our holy Mother Walatta-Petros herself would take turns: sometimes she would stay on Réma Island, other times she would stay at Afer Faras. But each morning she would go to Réma Island and supervise the construction of the church. In the evening, she would then leave and return to Afer Faras, spending the night there together with the sisters.

One day, while our holy Mother Walatta-Petros was in a boat, leaving Réma Island and returning to Afer Faras, a strong wind called *lagooni* suddenly arose. It propelled the boat and in an instant took it to Mahdere Sibhat. Those in the boat with her despaired of surviving, while those on the mainland, as well as those who stood on Réma Island, all loudly wailed out in unison, for it appeared to them that she would perish.

Our blessed Mother Walatta-Petros was not afraid or terrified, however, because she put her trust in God, the Lord of deliverance, who can do everything: nothing is impossible for God. Rather, she prayed in her heart the *Salama Malaak*. In addition, she sternly admonished those who were with her not to be afraid. At that very moment, the wind felt sternly admonished too, so the waves quieted down, and calm reigned. Thus, she could return to Afer Faras safe and sound and go home.

Our holy Mother Walatta-Petros continued to toil every day until the reconstruction of the church on Réma Island was complete. For instance, one day she went to fetch wood from Wondigé. Everything went as she had planned, and she returned safely.

Chapter 62: Our Mother Establishes an Order of Communal Life

[211]

Meanwhile, her community had grown immensely and reached the number of eight hundred. So Walatta-Petros established an order of communal life for them, compiling it from the holy books, from the *History of the Holy Fathers*, and from the *Canons of the Apostles*.

As the Acts of the Apostles says, "All those who believe shall live together, and all their possessions they shall have in common. They shall sell their assets and donate the proceeds to the poor. Every day they shall eagerly bind themselves to the house of worship as one in spirit. At home they shall bless the meal together, and eat their food joyfully and with a meek heart. They shall praise God," and no one among them shall say, "But this here belongs to me"; rather, it shall belong to all together.

The same circumstances prevailed in the time of our holy Mother Walatta-Petros. Everybody esteemed her highly, and she was feared and respected. Therefore, nobody would disobey her statutes. The members of her community embraced one another in love, like soul and body, brother with brother and sister with sister.

[212]

Nobody among them would say, "Only I eat, or only I drink, or clothe myself." Rather, they shared everything; even if it was only a single fruit, nobody would eat it alone. When they relaxed in the drinking place, if one of them received the cup, he gave it to his neighbor, saying, "You are thirstier than me, and I am in better shape than you are." While one passed it on to the next like this, the cup went around and would return to the first brother untouched. When, furthermore, community members went out on errands or to the market, be it brothers or sisters, those remaining behind in the morning bade them farewell in tears and in the evening received them back laughing joyfully.

Furthermore, our blessed Mother Walatta-Petros imposed a rule on the brothers and sisters that they should not go out one with one alone but rather in pairs of twos, be it to a place near or far, be it to the church or to the people of the town. And in the case that members of her community traveled to another town, she established that while on the road a monk should not eat at the same table with women, nor the nuns with men; and that a monk should not spend the night in a house where there was a woman, nor a nun spend the night in a house in which there was a man. She said to them, "It is better for you if the wild animals devour your flesh than that demons devour your souls and your bodies."

Her remaining orders were the following: that the members of her community should not speak loudly but softly; that they should not absent themselves as they pleased—be it even to receive the Eucharist or to the clothes' washing place—without properly taking their leave; and that they should not drink any medical potion. If they went to town, they should not eat there if they did not spend the night there. If they went to receive the Eucharist, they should not speak on their way, neither going nor coming. A healthy community member should not receive the Eucharist during the week, only on holy days. They should not shave their heads. Finally, they had to assemble for the prayer at meals, for the prayer upon retiring to sleep, and at any time at which the bell rang.

[213]

If anyone transgressed these orders, be it someone low or someone high in her community, she established forty whiplashes as the standard disciplinary measure against them. Eheta-Kristos

functioned as head of the community, second to Walatta-Petros;
Eheta-Kristos had authority over everything.

Regarding the community members, monks and nuns, they
were assiduously devoted to God. They had no other concern than
him, and submitted themselves under the feet of our holy Mother
Walatta-Petros. As for her, she guarded them like the pupils of her
eyes and watched over them like the ostrich watches over her
eggs. Walatta-Petros watched over their souls in the same way,
day and night. But every day she had to swallow ashes and dung
on account of them, just as our Lord had to drink bile and myrrh
when he tasted death for the redemption of the entire world.

Listen further, my loved ones! Lead weighs heavier than any   [214]
other load, but heavier still weighs putting up with the tempera-
ment of even one person! Our holy Mother Walatta-Petros said, "If
the community grew in number from its current size and increased
twofold, my heart would be able to carry it fully through the
power of God, my Lord, because I have been given the gift of patient endurance." Indeed, patient endurance is the first of all virtues, and the Kingdom of Heaven is obtained through it, just as the
Gospel says, "Through your patient endurance you will acquire
your souls."

Chapter 63: Praise for the Nun Qiddista-Kristos and Our Mother

How beautiful and sweet is the story of our holy Mother Walatta-
Petros! Neither honey nor sugar is as sweet as it is. For this reason,
it behooves us to love Qiddista-Kristos, who was rejected by our
people and regarded as lowly by all the sisters. Truly, Qiddista-
Kristos eagerly devoted herself to preserving Walatta-Petros's
story, and, burning with love for Walatta-Petros, compelled me to
write down this story and to reveal this treasure that lay hidden in
the field of the old people's hearts. So it is fitting that we remember
her, Qiddista-Kristos, and that we read the story of our holy
Mother Walatta-Petros. As our Lord in the Gospel says about the

woman who anointed him with fragrant oil, "Truly, I say to you, wherever this gospel is preached in the entire world, may they proclaim what this woman has done, and may they remember her!" O profound richness of God's wisdom, hidden to us! While many of our older ones were among Walatta-Petros's followers, God stirred up Qiddista-Kristos, who is younger than them all, and put his praises in her mouth. As scripture says, "Out of the mouth of children and infants you have made praise come forth."

[215]

Now it likewise behooves us to remember the virtues of our holy Mother Walatta-Petros, the sweet taste of her words and the fine speech of her lips. Truly, she spoke consolingly and persuasively, and did not impose herself with force. It was just as Peter says, "When you guard them, do not exercise control over them by force but rather through righteousness for the sake of God, without oppressing his people."

If, for instance, an angry brother came to Walatta-Petros in arrogance, the demon of anger and arrogance would leave him as soon as she put her hands on his shoulders and admonished him. Instantly, he would become gentle and humble, falling at her feet and saying, "I have sinned, forgive me!" Also, if a brother was possessed by the demon of fornication and lust, and revealed it to her, if she exhorted him and spoke consolingly to that brother, the demon would withdraw instantly, fortunately for the brother, and not assail him again.

Furthermore, if nobles came to her who wanted to renounce their worldly status, whether they were men or women, she did not impose great ascetic burdens on them, neither in terms of food nor drink, which they would have been unable to bear. Rather, she let them have what they required so that they would not run away and turn back to their old lives, for in their hearts they were infants. It was just as Paul says, "As is done for infants in the faith of Christ, I have fed you milk and have not given you solid food to eat because you are not strong enough yet. You are still living under the law of flesh and blood, not spirit." Our holy Mother Walatta-Petros acted in the same manner: she did not deprive them of any-

[216]

thing; rather, of their own free will, they quickly abandoned luxuries and adopted the ways of the community.

As for our holy Mother Walatta-Petros, when she sat down at table with the sisters, she would hold her nose when the various finely seasoned foods were served so that their aroma would not affect her: she despised it like the stench of excrement. For her a dish prepared with ash would be placed underneath the table, and she would eat it as if eating a proper dish together with the sisters.

Chapter 64: Our Mother Has a Vision of Father Absaadi

Furthermore, it behooves us to recall the vision that God revealed to our holy Mother Walatta-Petros when she was at Afer Faras and, standing in the church, recited the midnight prayers. In this vision, an angel of God seized Father Absaadi, the great monk and teacher of old, from Maguna Monastery. Guiding him, the angel ascended with him and took him all the way to the gate of the Seventh Heaven. There the angel of God stopped and said to Father [217] Absaadi, "Enter on your own, salute your Lord's throne, stand before him, and hear from him the words he will say to you! Truly, he has granted you permission to enter! But he does not allow me in, and thus it is not appropriate for me to pass through this gate."

At that moment, our holy Mother Walatta-Petros was seized as well, and she saw and heard this mystery through the words of the angel, that Father Absaadi's rank was higher than the angel's. Absaadi went to enter into the curtained chamber, while the angel stood outside.

She marveled at this and said, "Walatta-Maryam, have you heard this amazing and stunning thing that the angel has said to Father Absaadi, 'You enter on your own. But for me it is not appropriate to pass through this gate'?" Our blessed Mother Walatta-Petros said this while all alone; yet it appeared to her as if she was constantly speaking with Walatta-Maryam.

Meanwhile, there was a young woman who stood undetected near Walatta-Petros because the dark of night concealed her. Therefore, she could overhear this conversation through the words of our holy Mother Walatta-Petros, and later told it to us, so we have written it down. Since God wanted to make this vision known, he awakened the young woman so that she overheard this vision. It resembles the one written down in the letter of the Apostle Paul, who says, "I know a man who believes in Christ. Fourteen years ago, whether in the flesh or not in the flesh I don't know—only God knows—he was snatched up to the Third Heaven. I know this man. Whether he was snatched up in the flesh or not in the flesh, I don't know; only God knows. He was transported to paradise and there heard words that cannot be translated, and which mortal men cannot utter." Do you see the greatness of our blessed Mother Walatta-Petros, that she was granted this gift of hearing the mysteries of heaven while she was present in the flesh?

[218]

Chapter 65: Our Mother Drives Demons Away from a Royal Woman

Now we will further tell you about our holy Mother Walatta-Petros's great, awe-inspiring power: how the demons feared and fled her. One day, a great lady from among those of royal blood came to our holy Mother Walatta-Petros to pay her a visit. The princess met with Walatta-Petros, sat down in front of her, and the two of them conversed with each other for some time. Then our blessed Mother Walatta-Petros raised her eyes and saw demons amusing themselves with the princess and surrounding her entire body, like flies and mosquitoes surround a rotting carcass. When our holy Mother Walatta-Petros looked straight at the demons, they became terrified and took flight. Yet when she lowered her eyes to the ground again, they instantly swarmed back and surrounded the princess as before. But when Walatta-Petros again looked at them, they again took flight.

After the woman had left, Ghirmana asked Walatta-Petros about this matter because she had been with them. Ghirmana said to Walatta-Petros, "Please tell me what you have seen over that woman, because I saw you raising your eyes once and looking toward her, but then casting them down to the ground in embarrassment. Therefore, I have come to suspect that you noticed something."

Our blessed Mother Walatta-Petros indignantly replied to her, "What type of thought rises in your heart? I have seen nothing whatsoever over her!" Yet, Ghirmana again implored her. So Walatta-Petros then told her that she had seen demons, as we described earlier.

My loved ones, do you see how the demons feared our holy Mother Walatta-Petros and took flight from her? Truly, this recalls the saying of John Saba, the Syrian Spiritual Elder: "Just as jackals become scared and hide at the roar of the lion, so the word of the sage frightens the evil spirits and puts them to flight."

Chapter 66: Our Mother Cripples the Disobedient Nuns [219]

In accordance with this saying, we would like to reveal to you the gift of spiritual power that our holy Mother Walatta-Petros had been given. Among the young nuns, there was one named Amata-Kristos. She was charmingly beautiful and marvelously pretty; nobody in the world compared to her. One day our holy Mother Walatta-Petros saw her bragging and arguing with a companion. Instantly, Walatta-Petros summoned her and made her stand before her.

With an angry eye, Walatta-Petros looked her up and down and said to her, "What is it with this curviness of yours? What about attaining spiritual beauty instead through eating little food and drinking cold water? So far as I am concerned, I would like to pierce you with a spear and kill you!"

Walatta-Petros scolded her severely and then sent Amata-Kristos back to her house. Soon, then, Amata-Kristos fell ill with the piercing sickness. She remained ill for a long time, until her appearance had changed completely, with her flesh adhering tightly to her bones. She became paralyzed and never got up again.

Then there was another young nun like Amata-Kristos, named Eheta-Kristos. She became agitated as well and got it into her mind to go home to visit her relatives. Our holy Mother Walatta-Petros was then informed that Eheta-Kristos had become agitated. Walatta-Petros now summoned and questioned her. However, Eheta-Kristos concealed her thoughts from Walatta-Petros; she did not tell her. In addition, due to her great agitation, she refused to eat. So Walatta-Petros ordered that ashes be brought and mixed [220] into bread, which Eheta-Kristos forcibly was made to eat. Then she too fell sick and became paralyzed. For a long time, she lived crawling like an infant, due to the power of our blessed Mother Walatta-Petros. Eheta-Kristos never walked again.

Chapter 67: Our Mother and the Miracle of the Righteous Nun Ilarya

Through this door we have also found a path that leads us to the story of the saintly Ilarya. Recall that she is the one who had gone down to Zhebey with our holy Mother Walatta-Petros. There she had served her and done the cooking. Now, Ilarya had developed a strong affection for Saint Fasiladas the Martyr while living on Mitsillé Island with our holy Mother Walatta-Petros. Since that time, love for Saint Fasiladas had been instilled in her heart, and the chanting of his name had been written on her tongue so that she continually said, "Fasiladas!" As for Saint Fasiladas, he never parted from Ilarya and gave her success in her work so that her dishes turned out delicious-smelling and tasty. All day long, Ilarya would stand on the shore opposite Mitsillé Island, tapping her feet and chanting her song out loud, "O Fasiladas the saint, Fasiladas [221] the martyr, Fasiladas the strong, help me, come to him who is in need!" Straightaway, Saint Fasiladas then would come to her, and she would be so happy when she saw him, frolicking like a child who sees the faces of his father and mother. While alone, Ilarya would laugh as though she were with other people. She behaved like this every day. The place where she would stand was generally known, next to the cliff on the lakeshore of Afer Faras.

Whenever the sisters looked for her, they would find Ilarya engaged in such activity. They would marvel at her and ask her, "What are you saying, and with whom are you speaking?" But Ilarya would then change the topic and with her words would artfully and cleverly deceive them.

Meanwhile, our holy Mother Walatta-Petros always said to Ilarya, when the latter did the kitchen work, "Ask Walatta-Maryam whether she would like some stew, and do what she orders you to do!"

Every day Ilarya carried out Walatta-Maryam's wishes. One day she was charged as usual by her, and so she prepared the stew that Walatta-Maryam had ordered her to prepare. Then, when it had become evening, she presented the stew and placed it before Walatta-Maryam. But when God wanted to reveal Ilarya's great power, he instilled depression into Walatta-Maryam's heart so that she was disgusted by the stew and refused to eat it.

When our blessed Mother Walatta-Petros learned that Walatta-Maryam had refused to eat the stew, she said to Ilarya, "Why have you not cooked today as Walatta-Maryam wishes? Look, she refuses to eat!"

Ilarya responded, "Perhaps I should hurry and bring her something else." She then left, went to her house, and said to the women who were with her in the kitchen, "You women, prepare some fresh stew right away, and liberally add salt and all the spices appropriate for fish! Meanwhile I will go to a fisherman and buy a fish."

Then she took some grain, got a young servant girl to accompany her, and left in a hurry.

Now she saw that the sun had begun to sink and was about to set. Therefore, she said to it, "You, Sun, I implore you by the Lord of Saint Fasiladas to stand still and wait for me until I return, having carried out what I wanted to do." [223]

The servant girl said to Ilarya, "What are you saying? Are you really talking with the sun today?" However, she did not really comprehend what was going on because she was just a girl then.

Ilarya came to a fisherman then, bought a fish, and turned back in a hurry. Meanwhile the sun stood still as she had ordered it. After Ilarya had arrived at her house, she cooked that fish with great care, and taking it to the table, she put it before Walatta-Maryam, who happily ate it.

Meanwhile, Ilarya had forgotten about the sun; she just did not think about it. Thus, it kept standing still for quite a long time. The sisters marveled at this and said among themselves, "What has happened to the sun today?"

Then Ilarya remembered, went outside, and saw the sun standing still. Now she said to it, "Be blessed, Sun, because you have waited for me! Now, however, you have done enough: continue on your way." Right away, then, the sun set and complete darkness reigned.

The servant girl heard this, as well as the sisters who were with Ilarya. At that time, however, they did not understand what it meant, but only after Ilarya's death. The servant girl later told this episode to a priest, and he then told it to everybody.

Chapter 68: Our Mother Lives in Austerity

Now, though, it is appropriate for us to continue to reveal to you the story of our holy Mother Walatta-Petros. Truly, she spent all the days of her life wearing a dress of cowhide sewn together with sinew. At night, she spread out a palm-leaf mat and a sheepskin. She always slept like this, and never slept on a bed, nor did she ever put shoes on her feet. Furthermore, she had devices of sharpened iron manufactured for her that resembled bracelets with points and teeth like a saw, and she wore them on her arms and ankles. Finally, she covered her loins with sackcloth and always swept the ashes from the oven.

[224]

Chapter 69: Our Mother Speaks with Our Lady Mary at Amba Maryam Monastery

In addition, it is appropriate for us to recall what happened to our blessed Mother Walatta-Petros at Amba Maryam Monastery. One year, our holy Mother Walatta-Petros went to Amba Maryam Monastery together with a few of her community. Some of the rest of the community went to Bizaaba with Eheta-Kristos and spent the rainy season there. The others stayed at Afer Faras and were afflicted by great tribulation and distress because they had become orphans since Walatta-Petros and Eheta-Kristos were elsewhere. But our holy Mother Walatta-Petros spent the entire rainy season at Amba Maryam Monastery, by the will of our Lady Mary.

People knowledgeable about this matter have informed us accordingly, relating, "When our holy Mother Walatta-Petros wanted to return to Afer Faras, she went to the church in Amba Maryam Monastery, stood before the icon of our Lady Mary, and prayed, 'My Lady, I ask my leave from you, so allow me to return to my followers at Afer Faras.' But the icon stretched out a hand, seized Walatta-Petros by her gown, and spoke to her with these words: 'I won't allow you to leave me! Rather, I want you to spend the rainy season here with me.' This is why Walatta-Petros spent the rainy season at Amba Maryam Monastery. This did not please those who were with her, however. Instead, they grumbled because they did not know what the icon of our Lady Mary had said to Walatta-Petros.

"Our holy Mother Walatta-Petros addressed the icon in prayer again, asking Saint Mary to reveal the place where she should live. She said, 'My Lady, I beg you to reveal the place of my future home to me, the place that would please you as well as your beloved Son.' Now the icon took her by her hand and replied as follows, 'I implore you to not ever become restless and move from your assigned place! Don't say, "Here! There!" Go neither to the right nor

[225]

to the left. For your assigned lot is Afer Faras.' After having heard these words of our Lady Mary, Walatta-Petros became calm and ceased to be restless.

"In those days, a brother was with her, and he asked our holy Mother Walatta-Petros, 'Some of the community have gone to Bizaaba while we stay here. Why don't we join them?' She replied, 'No, we won't go—instead, they will come to us. You see, a man said to me, "Don't go!" ' So the brother asked her, 'Who is that man who said this to you?' Our holy Mother Walatta-Petros replied, 'I won't tell you his name. And if you disclose this matter and tell somebody else, that man will be very disappointed with me.' In reaction, the brother reassured her, 'I certainly won't tell anybody!' Now she made him swear that he would only disclose this matter after her death, and then told him that, as we have said before, it had been our Lady Mary who said this to her and who had implored her to stay."

That very brother is still alive now. He has told us about this encounter, and we have written it down.

Chapter 70: Our Mother's Brother Yohannes Dies

While our holy Mother Walatta-Petros was at Amba Maryam Monastery, through a vision she learned about the death of her brother Yohannes on the day he died in Tigré, before she was told about it.

[226]   Thereupon she sighed, "Woe, Yohannes, what has happened today!"

A few days later, Walatta-Petros was then informed that her brother Yohannes had died. She wept over him and mourned him greatly. Thus, the vision that she had seen turned out to have been true.

Meanwhile, Eheta-Kristos was in Bizaaba. From the time she had separated from Walatta-Petros, she wept and lamented continuously until she fell ill from depression.

After our holy Mother Walatta-Petros had heard about Yohannes's death, she descended from Amba Maryam Monastery in September, after the end of the rainy season, since the day of Yohannes's death had been September 8. She arrived at Afer Faras and reunited with those from her community who had remained there. Together with them, she mourned her brother and celebrated his memorial service on Réma Island. Afterward, she lived in Afer Faras.

A few days later, Eheta-Kristos also arrived from Bizaaba, together with those from the community who had been with her. She reunited with our holy Mother Walatta-Petros and wept with her over her brother Yohannes. Thereafter the entire community lived together again in Afer Faras, in one place.

Chapter 71: Our Mother Converts Walatta-Giyorgis Back to the True Faith

At that time King Fasiladas sent Walatta-Giyorgis, daughter of Queen Amata-Kristos, to our holy Mother Walatta-Petros so that she might convert her back from the faith of the Europeans and [227] teach her the true faith. All the Orthodox theologians had been unable to convert her back: the faith of the Europeans had burgeoned in her heart. When Walatta-Giyorgis arrived at our holy Mother Walatta-Petros's, the latter welcomed her, lodged her with herself, and taught her the true faith. However, even she was unable to convert her back at first.

Also, at that time, a sister named Fihirta-Kristos became restless and wanted to return to her region. Therefore, she said to our holy Mother Walatta-Petros, "Allow me to return home."

But our holy Mother Walatta-Petros implored her, "Just wait for a week. After that, I will let you go."

The sister replied, "Very well," and refrained from leaving.

When Walatta-Giyorgis refused to convert back from the faith of the Europeans, Walatta-Petros's entire community rose up against Walatta-Giyorgis and wanted to stone her. So our holy Mother Walatta-Petros took her and fled with her to Sadachilla, where Walatta-Petros went to the house of a nun and stayed there with Walatta-Giyorgis.

On that very day, the sister named Fihirta-Kristos fell ill; she then died the same week. Therefore, some sisters from Afer Faras went to Sadachilla to tell our holy Mother Walatta-Petros. Having arrived there, they stood at the gate. One Sadachilla sister who was there went outside, greeted them, and asked why they had come. They told her that Fihirta-Kristos had died. Having heard this, the sister went back into the house and told our holy Mother Walatta-Petros that those sisters had arrived.

Walatta-Petros replied, "Summon them." When they came to her, she asked them, "When did Fihirta-Kristos die?"

They replied politely, "She is alive and well, and not dead!"

But Walatta-Petros responded, "And yet I know she died yesterday!"

So then they admitted to her, "Yes, she has died."

Walatta-Petros gave praise to God then, and the sisters marveled that she had known about the death before they had told her.

Later, Walatta-Maryam came in, for she had been outside. Our holy Mother Walatta-Petros said to her, "Did you hear that Fihirta-Kristos has died?"

Walatta-Maryam was shocked and asked, "When did she fall ill? When did she die?"

[228] But our holy Mother Walatta-Petros said to her, "Don't be distressed! Through the power of God my Lord, it was I who killed her."

Do you see the power of our holy Mother Walatta-Petros, how she kills when she so desires, and how she knew before she was told?

Then, one day, while the two of them, our holy Mother Walatta-Petros and Walatta-Giyorgis, were alone in the house, a sister was cooking vegetables next to them because Walatta-Giyorgis liked to eat vegetable stew. That servant sister put the pot on the stove, lit the fire, and then left to go outside. Soon the liquid in the pot of vegetables boiled and spilled over. Immediately, our holy Mother Walatta-Petros got up, stirred the vegetables, and relit the fire that had gone out due to the spill.

When Walatta-Giyorgis saw Walatta-Petros's humility, she said to her, "You did this for my sake, didn't you? Now, due to your humility, I hereby convert from the filthy faith of the Europeans and enter your holy faith. Rejoice and be happy!"

When our holy Mother Walatta-Petros heard this good news, she fell to the ground and kissed Walatta-Giyorgis's feet. Then she rose up and ululated at the top of her voice, and all the sisters around ululated with her. On that day, there was great joy. Now Walatta-Petros sent a message with the good news to all the Lake Tana islands, and everyone rejoiced. They beat the drum and sang, "We praise God the praiseworthy to whom praise is due!" Also the king rejoiced, together with his court.

As the Gospel says, "If a woman has ten coins and one gets lost, will she not light a lamp, rummage through everything in her house, and diligently search until she finds it? And as soon as she has found it, she will call her friends and neighbors and say to these women, 'Rejoice for me because I have found my coin that had gotten lost!' I say to you: In the same way, there will be joy before God's angels because of a single sinner who repents." So behold the fruit of humility that springs forth from our Lord and was given to us, as he himself said, "Learn from me because I am gentle, and my heart humble. Then you will find rest for your soul." [229]

Many theologians, who interpret the books of the Old and of the New Testament, toiled and exhausted themselves for many years but were unable to convert Walatta-Giyorgis. By contrast, our holy Mother Walatta-Petros humbled herself and thereby became a broom for the filth of apostasy, converting Walatta-Giyorgis back in a blink. She reintroduced Walatta-Giyorgis to the true faith, just as our Lord, humbling himself and taking on the appearance of a servant, had returned man to his spiritual inheritance of old.

Chapter 72: Envious Monks Attack Our Mother's Authority

After that, our holy Mother Walatta-Petros returned to Afer Faras from Sadachilla and lived together with her entire community in one and the same place.

Some resentful theologians arose, however, giving vent to their resentment against our holy Mother Walatta-Petros with satanic [230] zeal when they saw that all the world followed her, that she was greater than and superior to them, and that they ranked below her.

Therefore, they said to her, "Is there a verse in the scriptures that states that a woman, even though she is a woman, can be a religious leader and teacher? This is something that scripture forbids to a woman when it says to her, 'Regarding a woman, we do not allow her to teach. She may not exercise authority over a man.'" With this argument, they wanted to make Walatta-Petros quit—but they did not succeed.

At that point, Father Fatla-Sillasé, the teacher of the entire world, said to them, "Did God not raise her up for our chastisement because we have become corrupt, so that God appointed her and gave our leadership role to her, while dismissing us? For this reason, you will not be able to make her quit. It is just as Gamaliel said in Acts, 'Leave these men alone and do not harm them. If what [231] they put forward is of man, it will pass and come to naught. But if instead it is from God, you will not be able to make them quit. Do not be like people who quarrel with God.'"

In the same way also, the resentful theologians were unable to make our holy Mother Walatta-Petros quit because God had authorized her. If her teaching had not been from God, her community would not have held up until now, but would quickly have disappeared. Through its continued existence, it is evident that her community is from God.

Chapter 73: Our Mother Provides the Miracle of Flour

Afterward, our blessed Mother Walatta-Petros lived with this community of hers in love and in peace. Even when they were afflicted and hungry, they did not think about nourishment for the body and did not say, "What shall we eat and what shall we drink?" but rather thought about spiritual nourishment, namely, fasting, prayer, love, humility, and other such things.

One day, a Friday, the food came to an end; there was none left at all. Even when they sought to borrow some, none could be found. When, as a result, Eheta-Kristos—for she was full of mercy and compassion for everyone—had lost all hope, she went to our holy Mother Walatta-Petros, stood before her full of sorrow, and said to her, "What will I do on the Sabbaths of Saturday and Sunday? Our sick will be dying of hunger, and I have absolutely no grain whatsoever in the storehouse. I have tried to borrow some by touring the region, but I was unsuccessful. Even if some grain [232] arrives tomorrow, can it be ground on the Sabbaths, or will our sick have to die of hunger?"

Our holy Mother Walatta-Petros replied, "O you of little faith! Are you not thinking these thoughts due to your hungry stomach? Tomorrow, though, you will witness God's power." Now Eheta-Kristos felt comforted and was full of faith.

Therefore, Eheta-Kristos then went to the kitchen building and ordered the women to prepare for the various cooking tasks. They were bewildered and said among themselves, "Where did she get the grain so that she can order us to get ready?"

Also, Eheta-Kristos sent the same orders to the monks. On the next day, then, men arrived from afar, bringing with them flour of various cereals, on nine donkeys. They handed the flour over to our holy Mother Walatta-Petros.

So she summoned Eheta-Kristos and said to her, "Take this which God has given us. Rejoice today, since you were worried yesterday!"

Now Eheta-Kristos praised God, took the flour, and gave it to the women who cooked. Likewise, she gave flour to the monks. Thus, they all had food to eat on the Sabbaths.

On another day, food was once again lacking in the same way. So Eheta-Kristos, who lent her services in the kitchen, asked Walatta-Petros, "What shall we eat for dinner tonight? Look, the grain has come to an end!"

Walatta-Petros asked, "We have no flour at all?"

Eheta-Kristos replied, "There is just one measure of flour." [233]

So Walatta-Petros ordered Eheta-Kristos to put that flour into the leather bag to make it ferment.

But Eheta-Kristos replied, "I won't put it into the large leather bag but rather into a small clay jar."

Yet Walatta-Petros said to her, "Don't be distressed; put it into the usual leather bag."

Eheta-Kristos obeyed, put the flour into the leather bag, and let it ferment. When the time came for baking, she thought that with so little flour she would only be able to bake enough for the few community members who were sick. Yet when she opened the leather bag, she found it full. So Eheta-Kristos went ahead and baked the dough, and it turned out as much as always. It sufficed for the daily meal for the entire community.

Chapter 74: King Fasiladas Enables Our Mother to Complete the Church on Réma Island

When, then, the reconstruction of the church on Réma Island was finished, our holy Mother Walatta-Petros sent the good news to King Fasiladas. In turn, he sent her fat cows, honey, clothing, curtains, and carpets. After that, following church law, she introduced the consecrated tabot, the representation of the Ark of the Covenant. In so doing, she made the people of Réma Island Monastery happy, as well as the others who had come from all the neighboring churches. This took place on July 9.

[234]   Afterward, Walatta-Petros dispatched people to the province of Tigré so that they would transport her brother Yohannes's remains and bring them to her. They did as she had ordered and brought the body to her. She received it and wept over it, then took it to the church on Réma Island and placed it in a coffin. Now our holy Mother Walatta-Petros said, "Last night my brother Yohannes came to me in a dream and said to me, 'Do not keep weeping over me and bothering me! Come and see my dwelling place in heaven: my lot is with the martyrs!' Then he took me

and showed me around. Thus, my heart was comforted, and I was happy."

Chapter 75: Our Mother Sees an Angel in Zhan Feqera

In those days, our holy and blessed Mother Walatta-Petros, together with a few from her community, set out for the town of Zhan Feqera and the house of Lady Walatta-Kristos to inspect an unsettled area well suited for living. Eheta-Kristos remained behind at Afer Faras. After reaching Zhan Feqera, Walatta-Petros went to Lady Walatta-Kristos's house and stayed with her. She there observed the Fast of Lent.

During that period, Maqdasa-Maryam fell ill. So our holy Mother Walatta-Petros went to visit her in the house in which she lay bedridden. While she was with Maqdasa-Maryam, 9:00 a.m. came. Thus, our blessed Mother Walatta-Petros covered her face with a cloth and began the prayer of that hour. As for Maqdasa-Maryam, she turned her face toward the west. [235]

At that moment, Layika-Masqal all of a sudden entered the house—without first having made his voice heard—because he was in service that month. Immediately, the Angel of God who was with our holy and blessed Mother Walatta-Petros drew his sword to strike him down because he had entered suddenly and disturbed her.

When the sick Maqdasa-Maryam noticed what was happening, she was upset and turned toward Layika-Masqal to rebuke him, "How dare you barge in at such an inappropriate time? Had it not been for Walatta-Petros, who saved you, a great tragedy would have happened to you. You only narrowly escaped death!"

Now our holy Mother Walatta-Petros removed the cloth with which she had covered her face and asked Maqdasa-Maryam, "What are you saying? What has upset you?"

Maqdasa-Maryam dissimulated, however, and responded, "But I didn't say anything."

Our holy Mother Walatta-Petros retorted, however, "Tell me the truth and don't hide anything from me!"

[236]   So Maqdasa-Maryam told her, "I saw the angel drawing his sword and getting ready to strike Layika-Masqal. But the angel then spared him on account of you."

This story became known throughout Walatta-Petros's entire community. The sick woman Maqdasa-Maryam ultimately died of that illness and was buried at Zhan Feqera.

Chapter 76: Our Mother and the Miracle of Butter and Cheese

In the same month, Lady Walatta-Kristos of Furé also fell ill. So she said to our holy Mother Walatta-Petros, "Bring me sour curd cheese because my illness has made me crave it." At that time, it was Passion Week.

Therefore, Walatta-Petros now dispatched messengers to the ladies and lords of the court at Gondar so that they would send her the cheese. Everybody there searched for it, but they found none, so the messengers returned and told Walatta-Petros this. Also, Lady Walatta-Kristos herself had searched for curd cheese but found none. Now, our holy Mother Walatta-Petros was distressed because she had not been able to find what the sick Walatta-Kristos craved.

[237]   Meanwhile, there was butter, not yet cooked or purified, in a big pot that had been sent by Lady Kristosaweet. On the evening before Easter, a sister dipped out a jar of that butter and purified it. With her was another sister who watched. The first sister then again dipped butter from the big pot and purified it. Then, at 9:00 p.m., that purified butter was found to have turned into curd cheese!

The first sister took some of it, looked at it, smelled it, and found its smell most pleasant, much better than the smell of ordinary curd cheese. So she said to her companion, "Listen, this butter has turned into curd cheese!"

The other sister replied to her, however, "Why are you lying and saying things that aren't so?"

The first sister retorted, "But I'm not lying, I'm telling the truth! If you don't believe me, take some of it yourself, look at it with your own eyes, and smell it with your own nose!"

Now her companion took a little of it, looked at it, smelled it, and it was just as the first sister had said. The two of them marveled at this, but left the curd cheese alone until morning. When the Easter fast was then broken and the time of the Eucharist had come, those two sisters prepared the food customarily required for that day and served our holy Mother Walatta-Petros some of that curd cheese.

When our holy Mother Walatta-Petros saw it, she said to the first sister, "Where did this curd cheese arrive from today, the cheese that for so many days we looked for but could not find?"

So that sister approached her and whispered in her ear, "The butter that was in the pot: half of it remained butter and half of it has become curd cheese!"

Now our holy Mother Walatta-Petros raised her eyes to the sky, [238] marveling and awestruck. She remained like this for a long time, praising God. Then she went and said to the sick Walatta-Kristos, "Get up and eat: what you craved has been found for you!"

Walatta-Kristos said to her, "Where did you find it?"

Our holy Mother Walatta-Petros replied, "God brought it to me because he saw my sadness and distress."

So Walatta-Kristos got up and ate that curd cheese. Our holy Mother Walatta-Petros also ate some of it and marveled at its fine taste and delicious smell.

At that time, elder monks from her community were there in that town of Zhan Feqera, as well as other monks who served under them. Walatta-Petros, by way of that first sister, sent the elder monks three bowls of that curd cheese, separately, and the same quantity also to the younger ones, separately, in their respective dining halls. Then that sister wanted to set out a second time to bring the monks some of the curd cheese but found that the rest had turned back into butter, reverting to its earlier condition.

When the sister saw this, she marveled and was awestruck. She then reported this miracle to our holy Mother Walatta-Petros, that the curd cheese had become butter again and reverted to its original state. When our blessed Mother Walatta-Petros heard about this miracle, she marveled at God's glorious deeds.

She then ordered that sister to go to the monks' dining hall and bring back the curd cheese that she had sent to the young monks so that it would be available for the sick Walatta-Kristos the next day and the day after. The sister set out immediately, hurrying at a run. She arrived at the monks' dining hall and impolitely opened their door with her own hand. She entered and found the bowls covered. She removed the bowls' covers, looked, and found them full, just as she had delivered them. She took two of three bowls and left and hurried back as she had come. She had not said anything, neither upon entering nor upon leaving.

When the younger monks later noticed the missing bowls, they were bewildered and said among themselves, "What is the secret behind this?" They did not know about the miraculous events that had taken place, neither about the earlier one nor about the later one. Those elder monks ate the three bowls of curd cheese that the sister had left them and marveled at its fine taste and delicious smell. For the younger ones, Walatta-Petros substituted another dish and sent it to them.

[239]

Later, this miracle was widely related and became common knowledge in Walatta-Petros's entire community. Those who ate from that curd cheese are still alive today. They are witnesses, and their testimony is true and no lie.

How plentiful and abundant are the stories about the miracles of our holy Mother Walatta-Petros! Behold, they cover the skies and fill the earth: nobody can conceal them. Can smoke be concealed if they lock it into a house, trying to hide it? Does it not waft out to be seen everywhere? Can even a small amount of olive oil be hidden if it is poured into the bottom of a jar? Even if lots of water is poured on top of it, in an attempt to conceal it, does the olive oil not rise to the top and gleam on the water? Likewise, we are unable to conceal the story of our holy Mother Walatta-Petros. Truly, it has spread over the length and breadth of all the lands!

Chapter 77: Why Our Mother Loved to Move Every Year

When King Fasiladas then heard that our holy Mother Walatta-Petros had gone to Zhan Feqera, and that Lady Walatta-Kristos had taken her in, he was profoundly indignant and distraught. He said to himself, "Is Walatta-Kristos better than me that she makes Walatta-Petros forsake my company for hers?"

However, our holy Mother Walatta-Petros had not gone looking for a different place on a whim but because her community in Afer Faras had compelled her, saying to her, "Let us travel to another place where we can till the land and produce food for our sustenance," since sustaining themselves at Afer Faras was difficult. Walatta-Petros herself did not want to stay in a single place either but liked to move each year from one place to another, like Abraham, Isaac, and Jacob, who had lived in tents. Our holy Mother Walatta-Petros did likewise and lived moving from one place to the next. [240]

When people would inquire of her—"What is it with you that you don't like to live in one place? All the saints like to fix a place for themselves! The Desert Fathers said, 'He who constantly moves from one place to the next is no real monk. He will not produce the fruit of good works; he resembles a tree constantly transplanted from one place to another so that it does not grow or produce fruit'"—our holy Mother Walatta-Petros would say to them in response, "I, too, am well aware that staying in one place is better than moving around. However, I do it for a particular reason. If I settled my sons and daughters in one place, they would there build a church, as well as houses for themselves. Then they would find rest from toil and labor, but through rest, the flesh flourishes, and from the flourishing of the flesh springs natural desire, and then Satan will assail them. If, however, I have them move constantly from place to place, and if they toil, and their bodies become tired and weak through hard labor and thinking of work, they will never give any thought to sin. When evening falls they will say, 'When will it be morning?' and when morning comes they will wish that the day was twice as long so that they can finish their work in greater leisure. So, that's why I do not like to remain in one place."

Chapter 78: Our Mother Goes to the Royal Capital and Falls Ill

After that, our holy Mother Walatta-Petros left Zhan Feqera and returned to Gondar. She stayed there for a short time, and found favor with King Fasiladas. Each day he would pay her a visit, for he cherished her and revered her as a great lady. When he went to see her, he would gird up his clothes like one of his soldiers. The ladies and lords of the court also would be submissive to Walatta-Petros with the utmost reverence.

While living in Gondar in this way, our blessed Mother Walatta-Petros became so sick from a violent illness that she was close to death. Consequently, the king, as well as all the noblewomen, were greatly alarmed. However, when Walatta-Petros was given water to drink from the washing of Jesus Christ's cross, she recuperated and promptly became healthy, on that very day.

Chapter 79: Our Mother's Friendship with Walatta-Maryam

Afterward, Walatta-Petros remained in Gondar for quite some time, such that the community grumbled against her. They said to Walatta-Maryam, "Was it not you who gave her this advice because you like to live at court?" With such talk, they aggrieved Walatta-Maryam, and she thought about splitting away from the community and returning to her home.

Then, when God's will allowed it, Walatta-Petros took her leave from the king. On that occasion, he gave her the district of Lag as a land grant and bade her farewell with great honor.

Our holy Mother Walatta-Petros then departed from court with [242]
Walatta-Maryam and reached Fintiro. Having arrived there,
Walatta-Maryam took her leave from our holy Mother Walatta-
Petros, saying to her, "As for me, I won't go farther with you, for
the community has grumbled against me because I offended them.
How can we—they and I—be at peace with each other in such a
situation? Therefore, I prefer to live in my hometown."

Our holy Mother Walatta-Petros replied to her as follows, "How
can you leave me in this town of Fintiro and separate from me?
Let's take our leave from each other after we have reached Qirinya. I will go on from there, while you can return home then."

Walatta-Maryam said, "Very well," and went on with Walatta-
Petros by boat.

Walatta-Maryam then arrived at Qirinya and there spent the
night together with Walatta-Petros. Our holy Mother Walatta-
Petros then once again asked her to keep going with her and accompany her to Fogera. She persuaded Walatta-Maryam to do so,
and they arrived at Fogera together. There, the two took leave of
each other in tears. Our holy Mother Walatta-Petros knew that
Walatta-Maryam would return that very day, however.

But for now, they kissed each other good-bye and separated,
climbing into their respective boats. Our holy Mother Walatta-
Petros covered her face with a cloth there and continued her journey. Walatta-Maryam turned toward her own journey as well. But
our holy Mother Walatta-Petros then began to pray to God that he
would make Walatta-Maryam return.

After Walatta-Maryam had traveled a little down the shore, fear [243]
and terror, agitation and despair suddenly gripped her heart, and
the lake became agitated as well. Now she said to the boatmen,
"For my good, take me back!" Having received her orders, the
boatmen turned around and poled back. As for our holy Mother
Walatta-Petros, she reached Damboza Island and spent the night
there.

Walatta-Maryam passed by, for she did not know that Walatta-
Petros had arrived on Damboza Island; rather, Walatta-Maryam
went on and reached Afer Faras. Our holy Mother Walatta-Petros

arrived at Afer Faras the next day. When she saw Walatta-Maryam, she laughed and was exceedingly happy.

Thereafter, Walatta-Maryam lived together with our holy Mother Walatta-Petros and did not separate from her until she died. All this happened due to the prayers of our holy Mother Walatta-Petros, for she did not want anybody to separate from her for forever.

Chapter 80: Praise for Our Mother's Humility

Once again, it behooves us to recall our holy Mother Walatta-Petros's humility. For she used to minister in the community when it was her turn, just like an ordinary sister. For instance, she would pour water for the washing of hands. At mealtime, she would have the sisters sit, but herself remain standing, and serve them; she would not sit down before the prayer of thanksgiving was finished. In addition, she would go into the kitchen, bake bread, and sweep up the ashes and rubbish, which she would carry in a basket on her head to throw away outside. Furthermore, she would brew ale, carry out the dregs, and pour them out at the usual place for such. There was no gate of humility through which our holy Mother Walatta-Petros would not pass; she could be found in every one. While she was a free woman, she became a maidservant. It was just as Paul says, "While I am free of all this, I have subjected myself to everyone."

[244]

One day—it was the Feast of Our Lady Mary's Assumption—Walatta-Petros held a great banquet and prepared many tables with all kinds of dishes and drinks. She then assembled all the sisters, old and young, seating each one at her place. Our holy Mother Walatta-Petros remained standing and ministered to them, pouring water for them to wash their hands, and making them happy. After the sisters had eaten their fill, she served them beverages, giving appropriate amounts to the old and young.

On that day she performed every work of humility, just as our Lord did at the Last Supper, when he washed his disciples' feet and said to them, "Do you understand what I have done for you? While you call me 'Our Master' and 'Our Lord'—and you speak rightly because I am indeed your master and your Lord—I have just washed your feet. Therefore, it likewise is right and behooves you, too, to wash your companions' feet. For I have given you my example so that you too will do as I have done to you." Our holy [245] Mother Walatta-Petros did the same and led the sisters toward the path of humility. As for them, they followed her and emulated her. If they transgressed the monastic order that she had established for them, be it in deed or in thought, this transgression lay open and was visible to Walatta-Petros, just like a small straw that has fallen into pure milk. Like a water torrent that streams down from a rooftop after a heavy rain, so the thinking of the entire community was visible to her. Our holy Mother Walatta-Petros said so herself, and many from among the sisters who can testify to this are still alive today. We know them personally.

Regarding the sisters, our holy Mother Walatta-Petros also prophesied that in later days, tribulations and downfall would afflict every single one of them. Unfortunately for them, the prophecy was fulfilled, and things happened as she had told the sisters. The sisters will testify to this as well.

There also were some from among the brothers and sisters about whom Walatta-Petros prophesied that they would leave and split away from the community. This was fulfilled as well; things happened as she had said.

Chapter 81: Our Mother Longs to Become a Hermit But Is Told to Stay

While our holy Mother Walatta-Petros lived in Afer Faras under such circumstances, a troubling thought assailed her, namely, that she had been deprived of the gifts of grace that she had been given in Waldeba while living there as a hermit. Therefore, our holy [246] Mother Walatta-Petros resolved to go to Narga Island and live there alone.

To this end, she came up with a pretext, saying, "Behold, many people have gathered around me, but I don't have anything at hand, neither clothes nor food. Furthermore, I cannot put up with the commotion created by so many people. Therefore, I will go to Narga because I want to live there: Get a boat ready for me! As for Afer Faras, Eheta-Kristos shall remain here because she has the capacity to put up with the commotion created by so many people and to live in such circumstances."

When our holy Mother Walatta-Petros spoke like this, Silla-Kristos responded, "Please don't act rashly! Let us pray first; let us pray for a week."

Our blessed Mother Walatta-Petros replied, "Very well."

The two of them then prayed for a week. Afterward, Silla-Kristos said to Walatta-Petros, "Please, tell me what you have discovered."

Our holy Mother Walatta-Petros replied, "Me? I have not discovered anything."

So Silla-Kristos said to her, "Let us pray for another week," to which she again said, "Very well."

[247]   So they prayed a second time like before, for a week. Then Silla-Kristos asked Walatta-Petros a second time, "Please, tell me what you have seen!"

Our holy Mother Walatta-Petros hid and concealed it from him, however. She said to him, "I have seen nothing whatsoever."

Silla-Kristos then said to her, "If you hide and conceal it from me, I will report it to you."

In response, our holy Mother Walatta-Petros said to him, "Go ahead then and report it to me!"

So now Silla-Kristos disclosed her secrets to her, according to what the Holy Spirit, the revealer of secrets, unexpectedly had given him to understand. He said to her, "The gifts of grace that are conferred when one lives in solitude as a hermit are different from the gifts of grace conferred in a community. To the hermit, all the varied gifts of grace are revealed, so that he finds comfort in them and does not stir from his place. By contrast, a community behaves according to its number, form, and shape. If you can put up with and patiently endure the behavior of an entire community, this is equivalent to the hermit's diverse gifts of grace."

Our holy Mother Walatta-Petros said to him, "You have spoken truly: it's because of this that I was restless. Now, however, our Lord has come and said to me three times, 'Tend my rams and my ewes, and don't be restless in the least! Did I not also say this to Peter before? Now I say the same thing to you as well.' Therefore, from now on I will not be restless."

Our holy Mother Walatta-Petros said this to Silla-Kristos, he then told it to us, and we have written it down. [248]

Furthermore, when Father Za-Sillasé said to our holy Mother Walatta-Petros, "Bless my clothes for me," she blessed them for him with the following words, "May God bless them for you, and may he make them like leather for you." Thus, they were blessed for him, and lasted for many years.

Chapter 82: Our Mother Survives Drowning

During the great famine in the year of the locusts, Abaala-Kristos gave Walatta-Petros a large amount of grain from Guna. Then, our holy Mother Walatta-Petros sent some of the community away to Guna so that they might find sustenance there during the months of the rainy season. The others stayed behind at Afer Faras together with our holy Mother Walatta-Petros. Later, she again sent away a few, from among those who had remained with her at Afer Faras, to live in Zambowl and sustain themselves on grain from Lag. Our holy Mother Walatta-Petros kept going back and forth: sometimes she was at Afer Faras, at other times at Zambowl.

One day, while Walatta-Petros was returning from Zambowl by boat, it capsized when she had almost reached Zagé. Our holy Mother Walatta-Petros fell and sank into the deep water. There she lay, having wrapped herself in her nun's leather cloak. She re- [249] mained there for quite some time, praying the *Salama Malaak* and the Lord's Prayer.

Those who had fallen into the water together with her quickly got out, but our holy Mother Walatta-Petros remained missing. Everybody was shocked and thought that she had died. When she had finished her prayers, however, she stirred in the deep, and then the lake's waters carried her and tossed her on the shore: She emerged safe and sound. Neither did her books perish; rather they emerged unscathed as well.

Thus, Satan was put to shame, who had wanted to endanger her and put her to the test. It was as Paul says, "I was in danger in the sea." After this, Walatta-Petros climbed into that same boat again and reached Afer Faras. There she lived for as long as it pleased God.

Chapter 83: Our Mother Establishes Her Seventh Community, at Zambowl

Later, our holy Mother Walatta-Petros left Afer Faras, and the entire community left with her, all of those who had remained in Afer Faras. Those who had gone to Guna returned. They all met at Zambowl and lived together in one and the same place, brothers and sisters, in their respective shelters and houses, and according to their respective monastic rules, one for each gender. This was the seventh community.

Walatta-Petros then reformed the monastic rule for monks: For meals and sleeping, she united the monks, youths and adults, in one building. Except for a few elder ones, nobody was allowed to [250] keep separate for any reason. By the will of God, she further chose Father Za-Hawaryaat from among them and made him their superior. In addition, she set apart those men who did manual work, in their own huts. She ordered them not to enter into the hut of any other for whatever reason. If they had any task that would take them there, they should stand outside and announce their business.

As for the sisters, she set them up in groups of fifty, and for each group of that number, each in its own house, there was one head woman. With these rules, the brothers and the sisters lived in love and in peace.

Chapter 84: Our Mother and the Miracle of the Candle

In those days, our holy Mother Walatta-Petros left Zambowl one Sunday night, and, with one sister, went to the church of Furé. She stayed in that monastery at that time. When our holy Mother Walatta-Petros wanted to read the Gospel of John during that night, while it was still dark, she sent the young woman to fetch her a lit candle. The young woman went to fetch it but kept searching for a long time for a fire because they had all gone out.

Meanwhile, a burning white wax candle descended from heaven   [251] to our holy Mother Walatta-Petros, and she began to read. After quite some time, the sister came back with a light but found our holy Mother Walatta-Petros with a light already, and reading the Gospel.

So the young woman inquired of our holy Mother Walatta-Petros, "I have been delayed by going around from house to house searching for fire. Who brought you this light?"

Our holy Mother Walatta-Petros looked at her indignantly, so the young woman immediately became quiet and did not repeat her inquiry. She now understood that the light had come down for Walatta-Petros from heaven.

Chapter 85: Our Mother and the Death of Amata-Dinghil's Son

Later, when our holy Mother Walatta-Petros again was at Zambowl with her original community, it grew there too: they became nine hundred. Then a violent illness rose up and struck against the sisters. It made them fall ill and killed many of them. Each day, two or three, or even more, were buried in a single grave.

Subsequently that illness reached the monks as well and began to kill them. Among the brothers there was a young man in the flower of his years whose name was Béza-Masqal, the son of our mother Amata-Dinghil. That young man had a handsome appearance; therefore, every time our holy Mother Walatta-Petros saw him, she wished for his death and implored God to receive him soon. Also, his mother kept praying for him likewise.

[252]

When forty days had passed since he had become a monk, Béza-Masqal spent Sunday not resting but girding his loins and, as it was his turn, serving the community at the midday meal. After he had finished his service, he fell ill on that very day and died on the third day after. The entire community was shocked.

Our holy Mother Walatta-Petros received a message informing her that Béza-Masqal had died. Before hearing about his falling ill, however, she had already learned about his death. Thus, when our holy Mother Walatta-Petros heard this news, she was very happy and praised God.

She then sent for Béza-Masqal's mother, summoning her. As for Amata-Dinghil, she did not yet know what had happened. She came before our holy Mother Walatta-Petros, who spoke to her in parables, saying, "When one obtains what one has wished and hoped for, must one be happy or sad?"

Béza-Masqal's mother responded, "One must be happy."

Our holy Mother Walatta-Petros replied, "You have judged well. Now, you too be happy and rejoice: Behold, your son, the heavenly groom, has found eternal rest."

Béza-Masqal's mother then said, "Who is this son of mine who has found rest?"

Our holy Mother Walatta-Petros replied, "Your son Béza-Masqal has found rest."

His mother asked, "When did he fall sick, and when did he die?" But then she sank to the ground in shock, losing her self-control, and wept for a time.

[253]

But our holy Mother Walatta-Petros scolded her and made her stop crying, saying to her, "Didn't you keep wishing to see his death? How can you now be sad? How can you change your mind and thus have lied to God? However, if you so desire, I will resurrect him for you."

Béza-Masqal's mother replied, "What has happened has happened. But allow me to go see him one more time."

In reply, our holy Mother Walatta-Petros said to her, "No, I won't send you. If you go, you will only cry there."

Amata-Dinghil replied, "No, definitely, I won't cry. Just send me for a short time so that I can see his face one last time before he is buried."

Walatta-Petros replied, "Very well, I allow you to go. But don't cry."

Now Amata-Dinghil left; the sisters who were her companions followed her, in tears, up to the gate of the wall of the monks' compound where Béza-Masqal had been laid out. When our holy Mother Walatta-Petros heard the sound of the sisters' crying, she became very angry and ordered that Amata-Dinghil be brought back.

Amata-Dinghil obeyed, returned, and said, "As for me, I didn't cry! Here, see whether there are tears in my eyes."

So Walatta-Petros sent her again, but had ten elder women from among her fellow sisters accompany her. Now Amata-Dinghil went to her son's dead body. She looked at him, hugged him, and kissed him. When the brothers saw her, they wept. After this, they took Béza-Masqal's dead body to the church with hymns and songs. Then, they read the *Book of the Dead* over him and buried him.

I ask you, my loved ones, if our holy Mother Walatta-Petros has ordered people not to weep over the dead like this, as you are witnesses, on what grounds do we have all this crying, this loud mourning, and these lamentations when community members [254] die? Do we want to defy our mother? Yet if we defy our holy Mother Walatta-Petros, we will defy Christ, according to what he himself said to the apostles: "He who disobeys you disobeys me, and he who disobeys me disobeys him who has sent me." Therefore, I, for one, believe it is incumbent upon us to observe the commands of our mother, for without such, we have no salvation. Also, Paul says, "We want you to know, concerning those who have fallen asleep forever, that you do not need to grieve over them like the other people who have no hope."

Chapter 86: Our Mother Sees Nuns Lusting after Each Other

On that day, after Béza-Masqal had been buried, Father Za-Hawaryaat went to our holy Mother Walatta-Petros and said to her, "How can we remain calm in the face of this deadly scourge that kills people out of the blue and gets worse every day? I, for one, think it would be best for us to conduct prayers and supplications with the *Praise of the Beloved* prayer book so that God might take this scourge away from us and show us mercy and clemency."

Our holy Mother Walatta-Petros replied to Father Za-Hawaryaat, "Don't worry! These deaths are no scourge but rather God's mercy."

Father Za-Hawaryaat responded, "As for me, I know of no such 'mercy of God.' Truly this is a scourge!"

Our holy Mother Walatta-Petros again replied to him, "But I tell you that this is God's mercy! It is not a scourge. How can you now contradict me and say, 'This is a scourge'?"

In reaction Father Za-Hawaryaat said to her, "So then, tell me about it and explain this secret to me so that I can believe your words."

[255] But our holy Mother Walatta-Petros replied to him, "No, I will not tell you. Rather, in your heart realize and believe that this is God's mercy."

Father Za-Hawaryaat responded, "No, I will not believe it unless you clearly explain it to me. I implore you by God to tell me!"

Now our holy Mother Walatta-Petros revealed the secret to him, "Since you compel me, listen up and let me tell you. It was evening and I was sitting in the house, facing the gate, when I saw some young nuns pressing against each other and being lustful with each other, each with a female companion. Therefore, my heart caught fire and I began to argue with God, saying to him, 'Did you put me here to show me this? I now pray and beg you to relieve me of the goods that you have entrusted to me. Or else take my life! I prefer perishing to seeing these sinful daughters of mine perish for eternity.'

"Instantly, God came to me and comforted me with the following words, 'Don't be afraid! I have heard your prayers and will fulfill your wish.' With him were seven black maidservants, namely, six strong young women in their prime and one elder woman. Then, he said to me, 'Take these maidservants so that they may carry out your wishes. Assign the six to the sisters' houses, one to each house. But the elder woman shall stay with you.' Then, everything happened to me as he had told me it would, and this is why I say to you: This is God's mercy. Won't you say likewise?" [256]

Now Father Za-Hawaryaat agreed, "It is indeed God's mercy."

In those days, 137 from among the brothers and sisters died. They traveled from toil to rest, from distress to happiness. May their prayers and blessings be with [manuscript owner's name] for eternity, amen.

A question came up: Her followers asked our holy Mother Walatta-Petros, regarding the brothers and sisters who had died, whether they were saved or damned. They said to her, "Please, tell us whether our hearts can be comforted and we need not doubt. All those who have recently died, are all of them counted among the righteous? Or are only some of them considered righteous, and others of them have been damned?"

Our holy Mother Walatta-Petros replied to them, "Nobody from among them will be condemned, nor anyone from my community before them or after them. Furthermore, not only the community members who are in my care but also those in the four corners of the world who invoke my name will be saved and not damned. But this, that which I say to you, does not happen due to my righteousness but due to God's mercy." [257]

Chapter 87: Our Mother and the Restless Nun

In those days, a sister named Fiqirta-Kristos, wife of Kifla-Maryam, became restless and decided to return home. Kifla-Maryam could not convince her to change her mind, neither through advice nor through admonition. He then told our holy Mother Walatta-Petros that Fiqirta-Kristos had become restless; he was distressed and wept because of her.

But our holy Mother Walatta-Petros consoled him, saying, "Don't be afraid and don't be distressed! Don't think she'll go away."

After Kifla-Maryam had heard this, he left Walatta-Petros a happy man. Then, through the prayers of our holy beatified Mother Walatta-Petros, Fiqirta-Kristos fell ill, passed away, and found rest.

Chapter 88: Our Mother Falls Ill and Is Visited by Angels and Demons

Afterward, on August 27, our holy Mother Walatta-Petros herself fell seriously ill. When the disease began to affect her badly, she was moved to the monks' quarters.

[258]   While she was bedridden there, angels came to visit her, bringing with them floral perfume from paradise that they drizzled into her nose. Then, when Silla-Kristos visited Walatta-Petros, he found her happy, thanks to the heavenly fragrance. He asked her, "What is making you so happy?" In response, she told him that which we have just related.

Then they moved Walatta-Petros again, taking her from Zambowl to the church of Furé and laying her down on a sickbed in the hut of a nun. While Walatta-Petros was there, her illness became even worse, and she almost died. So the community began to chant the *Praise of the Beloved* at the seven prayer times of the day. The entire community, brothers and sisters, cried out in woe and threw themselves down to thrash upon the ground.

One of the old men later related, "While we were chanting at 1:00 p.m., I saw the icon of our Lady Mary looking like a grieving woman. When the chanting was over, I went to our holy Mother Walatta-Petros but found her with a radiant face, happy and rejoicing."

Furthermore, Silla-Kristos reported, "After 9:00 a.m. had passed, I paid a visit to our holy Mother Walatta-Petros. While the two of us were talking among ourselves, she said to me, 'Today Satan came to me and tried to deceive me.' So I asked her: 'In what mode did he come to you?'

"Our holy Mother Walatta-Petros replied to me, 'He came to me in the guise of a luminous man, having split the house's roof to descend. In his hand, he held a censer, and from it wafted incense smoke as white as snow. It filled my mouth and poured down into my belly. That incense's scent was such that it robbed one of clear thinking. After him came a small child with a face radiant like the sun. In his hands, the child firmly held a cross of light. He approached me to bless me, but I withheld my face from him and threw myself down upon the ground. Yet there also I saw him. When I turned around, there he was as well. I turned right and left, but he was everywhere. Then he gave me a powerful blessing. But I asked him, "Who are you to bless me even though I don't want it?" The child replied, "I am the Son of God, and the one with the censer is a fallen angel." ' " [259]

Others further relate that our holy Mother Walatta-Petros reported, "Our Lady Mary came to me and said to me, 'I would have liked to give you rest from the toil of this world earlier, but the daily pleas of your sons and daughters roused my compassion. Therefore I let you stay in this world for a while longer, for their sake.' "

When our holy Mother Walatta-Petros knew that the time for her passing away had drawn near, she decided that she wanted to go to Réma Island so as to be buried there. So she said to the brothers, "Get a boat ready for me to go to Réma." They did as she had ordered them, and on September 30, about a month after she had fallen ill, she took her leave of the brothers and sisters, saying to them, "My illness has become grave indeed. Stay here, while I go to Réma. Farewell until we meet again, by the will of God!" [260]

At that time, Father Za-Sillasé said to our holy Mother Walatta-Petros, "Behold, my knees have become weak from standing in prayer, my throat coarse from chanting, and my eyes dim from the nights and days of incense smoke, which I have suffered continuously from when I began in the Church until now. I have no rest. Since those who see and hear loathe us, let it be done and enough! May we be spared this death of slow decay!"

Our holy Mother Walatta-Petros replied to him, "Do you want death to come now?"

Father Za-Sillasé responded, "Yes, I do."

So our holy Mother Walatta-Petros said to him, "If you want it, then let it be as you have said," and right away death struck, just as she had commanded it.

Chapter 89: Our Mother Prepares for Her Death

After that, Walatta-Petros was lifted into a boat and taken from Furé to Réma Island because she wished to die there and to be buried in the tomb of her father and her mother, just as Jacob had said to his sons when he was in Egypt, "Bury me in the tomb of my fathers." Also, Joseph had said as follows to his sons, "When [261] God will come to look after you, take my bones with you out of this place." For this reason, our blessed Mother Walatta-Petros said, "Take me to Réma." Having transferred her there, they lodged her in the house of one of the monks.

Thereafter, she forbade people to come see her, everybody except the priests Father Za-Mikaél and Father Silla-Kristos. With her stayed the woman Falaseeta-Kristos, who read the Psalms of David to her at night and the Gospels during the day. After 9:00 a.m., Father Silla-Kristos would always pay Walatta-Petros a visit to comfort her. On Thursday, November 20, four days until her passing away, Silla-Kristos paid her a visit, as was his custom, after 9:00 a.m. had passed. He entered her room and sat down before her.

Our blessed Mother Walatta-Petros then asked him, "Do you know who has been with me right now?"

He replied to her, "How can I know? But tell me what happened!"

So our holy Mother Walatta-Petros replied, "In this past hour, the 144,000 Children of Bethlehem whom Herod killed came to me and have been playing and enjoying themselves before me! But just now, when you arrived, they departed from me and left."

In addition, on that day, she summoned the abbot of Réma Island Monastery, Father Za-Maryam, as well as Father Kifla-Samaat [263] of Gond Monastery, and also all the brothers and sisters who were there. Our holy Mother Walatta-Petros then ordered that the *Comprehensive Book*, the *Rules for the Monks*, and other books be brought, and said to them, "Read!" So they read aloud all the books, chapter by chapter, where the rules for monks are written down.

After this reading from the books was finished, our holy Mother Walatta-Petros said to them, "I am clean of the blood of any person. Now, behold, I'm about to go to my Lord. Everybody who wants to follow the commands of these books should do so. But he who does not take heed, his sins shall be on himself! They will be none of my concern." After she had said this, she dismissed them, and they went back to their respective houses.

Chapter 90: Our Mother Is Visited by Christ and Made Archdeaconess

On the next day, Friday, Father Silla-Kristos again paid Walatta-Petros a visit, as was his custom. He entered and sat down before her. Our holy Mother Walatta-Petros then said to him, "Listen, let me tell you something: Today my Lord Jesus Christ came to me, wearing priestly vestments and shod with shoes of gold. His virgin mother came with him; she sat down before me, directly opposite from me. As for him, Christ leaned upon my bed and said to me [266] three times, 'He who has toiled and endured hardship in this world will be refreshed and live forever in the next. Truly, he will not see perdition!' In addition, our Lord breathed on my face and blessed me. So, I said to him, 'What is the meaning of this breathing on and blessing of me?' He replied to me, 'I have conferred upon you the rank of archdeaconess.'"

"This is what I have heard from her," said Silla-Kristos.

Chapter 91: Our Mother Appoints
Eheta-Kristos Her Successor

Then, on Saturday, when our holy Mother Walatta-Petros's illness became still more grave, everyone gathered in the church and made prayers and supplications. Great sadness reigned on that day. Also, at 3:00 p.m., Father Za-Maryam, Father Kifla-Samaat, Father Za-Mikaél, and Father Silla-Kristos assembled around Walatta-Petros and said to her, "When Moses passed away, he left Joshua in his place, who then watched over Israel. Also, Elijah left behind Elisha as his successor, and so did all great spiritual leaders in their respective times. Therefore, you too should now tell us, who will be mother in your stead and watch over your community?"

Our holy Mother Walatta-Petros replied to them, "In fact, I have ruled over them for many years. Didn't I time and again tell them: 'Serve!'? From now on, however, they shall be free, live as they see [267] fit, and watch over themselves. Who is the brother or sister whom I have not personally admonished and taught? Therefore, all of them are well taught and competent to take care of themselves.

"I say to you, however, that I entrust Eheta-Kristos to all of you. Behold, I am going and leaving her, while she remains behind alone. She will be disconsolate; she has no other hope than me!" Walatta-Petros said this to them three times. After she had said these things, she dismissed them. In this veiled manner, she had thus indicated to them that they should appoint Eheta-Kristos as abbess.

Chapter 92: Our Mother Departs to Eternal Life

After this, the suffering of our holy Mother Walatta-Petros became intense, and she was no longer able to speak. So the door to her house was closed and nobody was allowed to enter. Everybody gathered in the church in the evening, staying into the night to chant supplications and say prayers.

Then, when it was midnight on the turn to Sunday, November 23, Walatta-Petros's soul left her body and she passed away in peace when she was fifty years old, of which she had spent twenty-four before her repudiation of the world and twenty-six after it. On that day, a column of light was planted that appeared to all the world.

All the people from all the Lake Tana islands and from all the neighboring regions now assembled, because Walatta-Petros had been a mother to them in many ways. To him who had looked for instruction, she had given food and clothing, and assigned him to a teacher. The assembled wept over her and wailed over her, intensely and loudly, just as the children of Jacob had wept and wailed over him. O such weeping and wailing! O such cries of woe and shouts of pain! On that day, nobody looked at his neighbor; everybody was so grief-stricken that none could console. On that day, the monks could not be distinguished from the laypeople because their monks' caps had been cast from their heads by rolling about in grief.

[268]

After this, during the singing of psalms and hymns, Walatta-Petros was shrouded in a nun's leather cloak, according to the rules of monastic life, and buried near the church entrance; she was put in the ground without a coffin.

May her intercession be [with the patrons of this manuscript,] with the sinful scribe, and with all of her sons and daughters who have longed for and been anxious for this *Life and Struggles* to be written down. For eternity, amen.

[One of the Twenty-Seven Miracles:] The First Miracle: How Our Mother Replenished the Batter

[273]

In the name of the Father, the Son, and the Holy Spirit, one eternal God! We will now continue by writing down the miracles that our holy Mother Walatta-Petros performed; may her intercession be with [manuscript owner's name] for eternity, amen.

Listen and let us tell you about the powerful miracles that happened after our holy Mother Walatta-Petros had passed away. We have heard them and seen them! Many took place on the days of her memorial services, from the thirtieth-day memorial service until that of the end of the year, when God's blessings descended on all the memorial service works.

On those occasions, many people would gather, in countless numbers, from the islands and the monasteries, from the churches and the monastic settlements, from all the provinces. Among them were abbots, priests, deacons, and monks, with incense burners and crosses; there were the poor and the wretched, and the blind and the lame, because Walatta-Petros's fame had spread to the ends of the world. They all were given plenty of food and drink, according to their ranks and needs, until they were so sated that they left some of it untouched.

[274]

The first miracle that happened at the time of a memorial service for her:

People relate that, in a big jar, there was a little bit of leavened batter—enough for only one piece of flatbread—that was left over from the memorial service. But then that batter boiled up and filled the jar to its brim, spilling over. When they then poured it out, the batter did not decrease or diminish. On the contrary, it increased anew each day, and the jar was always full again. As for the sisters who knew about the batter's secret, they kept quiet and did not speak about it; rather, they marveled at the great power of our holy Mother Walatta-Petros.

But then one of the other sisters, who habitually spoke rashly, came and looked at the boiling up batter, shouting out, "Look at how this batter boils up!" Immediately, it quieted and ceased to boil up. Then, when the sister cooking scooped some batter out, the remaining batter began to shrink and diminish from its former abundance.

Also, the sisters' small quantity of flour increased likewise, so much so that they could take many measures from it, just as the

prophet Elijah had done at Sarepta. But when another sister spoke [276]
up too, the flour diminished likewise. Truly, he who is rash to
speak drives God's blessings away!

Regarding this, the Apostle James says, "Each man should be
quick to listen and slow to speak." In addition, John Saba, the Syrian Spiritual Elder says, "The Creator keeps his distance from him
who is rash to speak." Furthermore, it is said, "A small load of wood
is more than enough to bake a great deal of bread between evening
and morning."

Regarding the further blessings that happened to the bread, the
stew, and the ale at each memorial service, they are innumerable:
I don't know them all—but God knows. All this happened through [277]
the power of our Mother Walatta-Petros. May her prayers and her
blessing be with [manuscript owner's name] for eternity, amen.